Anita Schroven

Women after War

Spektrum

Berlin Series on Society, Economy and Politics in Developing Countries

edited by

PD Dr. Dr. Ulrich van der Heyden (Department of Theology, HU Berlin)
Prof. Dr. Volker Lühr (Institute of Latin American Studies, FU Berlin)
Dr. Ulrike Schultz (Institute of Sociology, FU Berlin)
Prof. Dr. Manfred Schulz (Institute of Sociology, FU Berlin)

Volume 94

LIT

Anita Schroven

WOMEN AFTER WAR

Gender Mainstreaming and the Social Construction of Identity in Contemporary Sierra Leone

LIT

This book was printed with the financial support of the Max Planck Institute for Social Anthropology in Halle/Saale.

Bibliographic information published by Die Deutsche Bibliothek
Die Deutsche Bibliothek lists this publication in the Deutsche Nationalbibliografie; detailed bibliographic data are available in the Internet at http://dnb.ddb.de.

ISBN 3-8258-9627-7

A catalogue record for this book is available from the British Library

Auslieferung/Verlagskontakt:
Fresnostr. 2 48159 Münster
Tel. +49 (0)251–62 03 20 Fax +49 (0)251–23 19 72
e-Mail: lit@lit-verlag.de http://www.lit-verlag.de

Distributed in the UK by: Global Book Marketing, 99B Wallis Rd, London, E9 5LN
Phone: +44 (0) 20 8533 5800 – Fax: +44 (0) 1600 775 663
http://www.centralbooks.co.uk/acatalog/search.html

Distributed in North America by:

Transaction Publishers
New Brunswick (U.S.A.) and London (U.K.)

Transaction Publishers
Rutgers University
35 Berrue Circle
Piscataway, NJ 08854

Phone: +1 (732) 445 - 2280
Fax: + 1 (732) 445 - 3138
for orders (U. S. only):
toll free (888) 999 - 6778
e-mail:
orders@transactionspub.com

Table of Contents

Acknowledgements

I thank my supervisors Brigitta Hauser-Schäublin and Ulrich Braukämper (University of Göttingen) for their academic support and encouragement throughout my research and in the process of writing up my master thesis.

Jacqueline Knörr (Max Planck Institute for Social Anthropology) engaged in constructive intellectual debates on my thesis and provided the strategic support crucial for this publication.

I am indebted to Florence Butegwa, Jebbeh Forster (both UNIFEM) and Desmond Molloy (formerly UNAMSIL) for providing me access to the local offices of the United Nations and for deepening my understanding of women's lives in post-war Sierra Leone.

I owe the greatest gratitude to those Sierra Leonean women and men who shared their personal experiences of life during and after the war with me. In many cases recalling and recounting caused grief and frustration and in many cases I was deeply impressed by the courage and confidence which nevertheless prevailed and which I hope to convey in the pages that follow.

The fieldwork in Sierra Leone was enabled by a grant of the Friedrich Ebert Foundation. The Max Planck Society for Social Anthropology provided the financial means for publication. I thank Jutta Turner for carefully copy-editing this book.

List of Acronyms

AFRC	Armed Forces Revolutionary Council (Sierra Leone)
APC	All People's Congress
CDF	Civil Defence Forces
CEDAW	Convention for the Elimination of all kinds of Discrimination Against Women
CivPol	UN Civil Police
COOPI	Cooperazione Internazionale (Italian INGO)
CVT	The Centre for Victims of Torture (INGO)
DDA	UN Department for Disarmament Affairs
DD(R)R	Disarmament, Demobilisation, (Rehabilitation) and Reintegration
DPKO	UN Department of Peacekeeping Operations
ECOMOG	Economic Community of West African States' Monitoring Group
ECOWAS	Economic Community of West African States
FAWE	Forum of African Women Educationalists (African INGO)
GTZ	Gesellschaft für technische Zusammenarbeit (German INGO)

IDP	Internally Displaced Person
INGO	International Non-Governmental Organisation
IP	Implementation Partner
IRC	International Rescue Committee (INGO)
MilObs	UN Military Observers
NCDDR	National Commission for Disarmament, Demobilisation and Reintegration (in Sierra Leone)
NCDDRR	National Commission for Disarmament, Demobilisation, Rehabilitation and Reintegration (in Liberia)
NGO	Non-Governmental Organisation
NNGO	National Non-Governmental Organisation
NPFL	National Patriotic Front of Liberia
NPRC	National Provisional Ruling Council (Sierra Leone)
OCHA	UN Office for the Coordination of Humanitarian Affairs
OSAGI	UN Office of the Special Advisor to the Secretary-General on Gender Issues and Advancement of Women
PRIDE	Post-conflict Reintegration Initiative for Development and Empowerment (NNGO)
RUF/SL	Revolutionary United Front of Sierra Leone
SALW	Small Arms and Light Weapons

(S)GBV	(Sexual and) Gender Based Violence
SRSG	Special Representative of the Secretary General (United Nations)
TRC	Truth and Reconciliation Commission
UNAMSIL	United Nations Mission in Sierra Leone
UNDP	United Nations Development Program
UNFPA	United Nations Fund for Population Activities
UNHCR	United Nations High Commission for Refugees
UNICEF	United Nations Children's Fund
UNIDIR	United Nations Institute for Disarmament Research
UNIFEM	United Nations Development Fund for Women
UNIOSIL	United Nations Integrated Office for Sierra Leone
UNMIL	United Nations Mission to Liberia
UNTAG	United Nations Transitional Assistance Group (Namibia)
UNSG	United Nations Secretary General

1 Introduction

Wars don't simply end, and wars don't end simply (Cynthia Enloe).

Cynthia Enloe captures a notion often forgotten in the analysis of conflict and war, the fact that with a peace treaty signed and open warfare ended, the war and its results and influences are far from over. It is only the beginning of a different struggle, re-establishing life, communities, governance, economies and infrastructure, re-integrating those who fled the war and those who have been participating in it. Of cause many more dimensions can be added. In itself, these are enormous tasks, let alone in an unstable and politically charged post-conflict situation. Besides political powers having been contested, lives and the every-day of the people are affected by the war. The challenges faced during the war have their effects in its aftermath and thereby influence the way societies at large and specific communities can (re-) establish themselves.

The situations in which women find themselves as individuals and as part of these communities are not only influenced by their pre-war lives but also by the ways they were affected by or participated in the war. Yet, with the signing of a peace accord, the combatants do not instantaneously turn into civilians. They face specific challenges, having to adapt to new circumstances with their past war-involvement affecting their possibilities to establish new lives. Often, these instances are considered to be the actual peace processes, with the integration of former combatants into the wider society occurring as part of a long-term peace building effort.

With the end of the Cold War the involvement of the international community, institutionalised in the United Nations, into national and interstate conflicts increased (Katayanagi 2002: 37ff.)[1]. Simultaneously the analysis of intra-state conflicts shifted to the issue of degenerating or "failed states". The response to these categories of analysis is a broad-based inter-

1 For the numbers and locations of current missions, see <www.un.org/Depts/dpko/dpko/bnote.htm>.

vention and reconstruction approach, using the UN Charter more freely and including peace building and –keeping elements into a so-called multidimensional UN mission (Debiel 2002: 475ff.)[1]. Considering the multi-layered and deep effects a war can have on societies and its institutions, many of these reconstruction activities concentrate on (infra-) structural matters. Other spheres are neglected, while again some areas would be difficult to support from the outside, such as the social and cultural dimensions of war as well as their effects on the people.

The present work shall explore these relations on the background of the Sierra Leone post-war situation and the Disarmament, Demobilisation and Reintegration programme (DDR) for the former combatants of the eleven-year civil war. From an anthropological as well as an interdisciplinary perspective, I investigate the multi-layered interrelations between the organisations involved and the people their programmes are supposed to be designed for. In the present context the focus shall lie on women formerly involved in the war, and the ways Demobilisation[2] offered them options or support to enter into civilian life[3].

Furthermore, the developing discourse on the effects of war or armed conflict can have on women specifically and gender relations on a broader basis shall be included into the analysis as the overarching theme. Especially discussions by women's rights' activists describing perceived changes due to war-time influences regarding women's enlarged responsibilities in a war situation or even propose women's empowerment happening through direct participation in combat. These ideas may influence the way organisations implementing DDR and related projects accommodate women, combatants and women combatants.

1 See also Osman (2003); Zisk Marten (2004).
2 In this book, Demobilisation (with a capital 'D') will be used synonymously for the acronym DDR.
3 While it is contestable, whether in a militarised society "civilian life" is possible, in the present work, it shall mean the non-combat situation of the wider population in which ex-combatants are supposed to participate after the war.

1.1 Preface

The topic

As part of the international community's physical intervention into conflict-laden situations, the DDR programme is designed to support a long-term peace process by increasing public security through assistance to fighters after long years of battle to return to civilian life. This is part of a broader framework supporting institutions with the aim to stabilise peace. Such a programme was designed and implemented by the government of Sierra Leone, under close cooperation with the UN peacekeeping mission and other UN and non-governmental organisations (NGOs).

Considering the social and cultural effects on people, dimensions of gender relations may be influenced by a war. Women participating in the conflict are supposed to be directly exposed to such changes. These presumably have an impact on the situations women find themselves in after the war and the ways they might react to the programmes offered to them. Amongst them is DDR, representing the one programme in which only combatants are directly addressed. In this thesis it is the core process around which the discussion revolves because it is a crystallising point for many measures in a post-conflict setting that revolve around women, combat and the attitudes organisations hold towards them. Whether institutionalised in gender mainstreaming or in assumed changes of gender roles during the war, the way DDR is implemented and the way staff is addressing the women in question shall be closer examined to reveal these attitudes.

At the same time women emerging from combat have their own expectations and ideas on how their lives are to develop in the evolving peace process. Faced with the DDR programme, their reactions and following decisions to participate or react otherwise shall be the next point of interest. Emerging out of a war that affected all its participants, the question is whether the programme is adequately addressing women combatants in their post-conflict situations and what kind of ideas, notions and presuppositions are included in the programmes in which the women are engaged. With the organisations involved being obliged to implement gender mainstreaming policies with notions of gender equality and equity inherent to them, the consecutive question is how women combatants react to these. How do such policies and their implementation influence their perception of the programme and, more importantly, their perception of themselves? Underlying this aspect is the interaction between programmes, organisations' staff and the intended participants.

The above questions shall be analysed on the basis of fieldwork done on the Sierra Leonean post-war situation and the Disarmament, Demobilisation and Reintegration programme. Having been introduced by the national government, this programme was influenced by political interests, yet at the same time it was facilitated by the United Nations and other institutions of the international community. Due to organisational interrelations and funding mechanisms, their guiding perceptions are the main reference points to which other organisations adhere.

The DDR programme of Sierra Leone appears to be an appropriate reference point for such investigations as it is "deemed as the most successful of a UN supported peace process" (Molloy 2004: 16). At the same time, it received substantial criticism along with many other DDR programmes for not making any lasting impact on its participants. On a similar note, the programme is being either criticised for the way it ignored women combatants, failing to adequately address them (Puechguirbal 2003a: 24), on the other hand having neither positive nor negative effects on women's potential integration after passing through the process (Weinstein and Humphreys 2005: 1, 22). While the Sierra Leonean programme was claimed to be "gender neutral", it attained a reputation of "gender blindness"[1].

Rather than analysing why Demobilisation in Sierra Leone "failed women", this book will focus on the effects the project and its surrounding activities had on women in the understanding of "gender neutrality". In this light, relevant UN mechanisms and concepts such as gender mainstreaming shall be taken as the reference point in the Sierra Leonean context of post-war peace building and demobilisation. Despite or because of allegations of being "gender blind", organisations and programmes still have effects on different groups within the local population, either by including or excluding them in certain ways. These ideas shall be analysed to show the kind of impact the programme had and continues to have on women who had fought in the war.

---

1 See, amongst others, Mazurana and Carlson (2004); Farr (2003b).

Conceptual positioning

> That we need to talk about "women and war" underscores the gendering of our construct of war [...] Women are denied agency, made present but silenced. Perhaps that is why so many feminist researchers [...] focus on the subject of women and war. Perhaps our scrutiny is a fascination for the forbidden. Perhaps we need to reclaim an erased identity, to legitimise our ability to speak, to tell our own "war stories", to claim an "authentic voice" (D'Amico 1998: 119).

The issues surrounding "women and war" have received more and more attention after the end of the Cold War. This may be part of a growing desire to understand social and cultural processes and consequences of wars, as their explanation can no longer be embedded into that larger political framework. Parallel to international bodies such as the UN adopting resolution 1325 on women, peace and security in the year 2000 or the Convention for the Elimination of all kinds of Discrimination Against Women (CEDAW) being ratified by more state governments, the topics have gained the attention of different academic areas. In the above quote, D'Amico points out that this perspective is not self-evident but had to evolve in a broader discourse in which "feminist researchers" played a great part in developing and furthering the discourses on the topic. She further sheds light on the fact that the whole field of research is very much embedded in a gendered understanding of both war and women as participants and as researchers. Endeavouring to break out of these assigned roles might be one reason why it is often women exploring these topics that had previously received much less attention from a feminist or women's rights perspectives. Women's prerogative associations with peaceful behaviour and victimhood in conflict situations are broken up to reveal their aggressive and violent potentials. Yet, as Tickner points out, scholarship of women and war cannot stop with revealing the gender constructs of war and violence in a society. If so, they would continue failing to explain the sources of violent conflict (Tickner 1999: 11). Nonetheless, she also points to the fact that by deconstructing war-related gender stereotypes, women's other confinements could be broken up and thereby they would have "their credibility as actors in matters of international politics and national security" asserted (p. 4).

These notions might explain why many analysts wish to see war's repercussions as a change in women's lives, breaking up established roles and leading women to change or challenge social and behavioural patterns. With such changes, some analysts presume potential shifts of self-perception and even gender roles occurring during the wartime and that these effects may continue to influence the situation of women after the conflict[1]. Parts of the literature in this field convey a notion of an expected or even presumed empowerment of women by their war experiences.

The authors above and many more, such as in the book edited by Afshar and Eade (2004), claim that it is the post-conflict moment where outside interventions should strive for the empowerment of women, thus supporting the positive changes assumed to have occurred during the war. With support from the outside, the "backlash" into pre-war gender relations could and should be prevented. These ideas are not confined to the academia but enter the field of post-conflict work. In this context, perceiving changes and subsequently supporting them belongs to the mandate of some agencies and to the obligations of others, relating to international conventions or gender mainstreaming plans. Here, women's equal rights are emphasised and gender mainstreaming as a tool and implementation target at the same time pushed to achieve this goal.

While elaborating gender, which includes the socially constructed roles and resulting perspectives of women and men, an unfortunate conflation of women and gender happens too often, both in academic and development discourses (Mazurana and Carlson 2004: 13). This not only limits the perspective that the concept of gender is supposed to widen but also omits the chances its introduction as a working concept would have enabled. Despite the need to investigate topics relating to women during armed conflict employing gender-related notions, men in the same circumstances should not be forgotten either. There are needs for research on masculinities and their changes due to conflict as well (Mazurana et al. 2002: 110)[2].

The title of this book sets out to capture the spectrum of potential effects discourses and their manifestations in different projects have on women in a post-conflict situation. With this perspective, gender mainstreaming signifies a concept in the discourses depicted above as well as programming tool for organisations. As such, it should not only be perceived as an instrument em-

---

1 See, amongst others, Meintjes et al. (2001); Seifert (2004); Turshen and Twagiramariya (1998).

2 See also Hagemann-White and Lenz (2004); Kimmel et al. (2005); Morrell (2001); Zarkov (2001).

ployed by international organisations but as a crystallising point at which the mechanisms, power relationships and basic principles of discourses around the issues of women, gender and gender relations may be analysed[1]. At the same time the title hints at the limits of such interventions, which are explained by the ways women are embracing these ideas and interpreting them, based on personal experiences, to become parts of their self-images. In doing so, these women make choices and turn categories put forward by the international community into realities of their own, individual interpretation.

After setting the topic and with the theoretical background of the work briefly introduced, the use of a few central terms shall be contextualised shortly.

Gender, as a social construct of meaning attributed to physical differences, shall most of the time not be conceptualised in isolation, but in relation to other social matters, such as gender roles. According to El-Bushra, these are "activities that men and women are expected to carry out", which may differ according to socio-cultural circumstances. Similarly, gender identities will be used to describe "idealised characteristics and behaviours of different sexes" which can be differentiated further by other dimensions such as age, social status or economic situation (El-Bushra 2004: 171).

The notion of gender as a socially constructed category based on sexes is transmitted into the definition of gender mainstreaming as put forward by many UN organisations:

> Mainstreaming a gender perspective is the process of assessing the implications for women and men of any planned action, including legislation, policies or programs, in all areas and at all levels. It is a strategy for making women's as well as men's concerns and experiences an integral dimension of the design, implementation, monitoring and evaluation of policies and programs in all political, economic and societal spheres so that women and men benefit equally and inequality is not perpetuated. The ultimate goal is to achieve gender equality (DAW 2000: 2).

The above quote reveals the challenge that mainstreaming any concept into all areas of work poses to policy makers and practitioners. At the same time it exposes the implied perceptions of gender within the broader concept of

---

1 See, amongst others, Bereswill (2005); femina politica (2004); Goldstein (2001); Wichterich (2005).

gender mainstreaming. On this background Bereswill points out that the definition of gender as a constructed and flexible category, by explicitly including all possible diversities within the concept of gender, may blur the realities of the underlying inequalities and discriminations women face in their every-day life. They are actually being reduced and downplayed to mere role-driven behavioural patterns, which then are perceived to be comparatively easily changeable and therefore pose less of a problem (Bereswill 2005).

When talking about women, the age standard set by international organisations is a female person above 18 years. With an average marriage age of 15.5 years for girls in rural Sierra Leone (Richards et al. 2004: 5) and the following life as wives and mothers, this legal definition of adulthood seems inappropriate within the current perspective. Given life's circumstances, especially under conditions of war, young people experienced the realities of otherwise adult-associated life at a very early age and distinctions between childhood and adult life often seem to disappear in the war (Nordstrom 1996: 404; McKay and Mazurana 2004: 119). Therefore, this work does not restrict itself to an age-based definition of women. Instead, it includes those girls who cannot be regarded as children any more.

In the following theoretical conceptualisations, the terms identity, agency and actors will become relevant. Drawing on Moser and Clark (2001a), rather than being synonymous with the individual, actors are "socially constructed" within social relationships and equipped with specific knowledge and capabilities, thereby determining an actor's agency. In this notion, agency is understood in the similar way as identity, both being immersed into "multiple realities", social relationships, which are constantly changing and being redefined. Therefore, they can be assumed to change over time in various settings as well as social contexts (Moser and Clark 2001a: 5). While interdependent, agency and identity can be differently constructed and interpreted by different actors in their respective situations, leading the individuals to cope with their environment in certain ways.

Already in the introductory part, the term combatant has been used. The title may seem an unusual choice and in some circumstances awkward to use, for example when talking about a regular army. It is the values inherent to other words like fighters, soldiers or rebels, linking the terms to inclinations of organised or irregular, voluntary or mercenary, legitimate or rebellious that can be avoided by restricting the vocabulary to combat and combatant for those participating under various circumstances. These circumstances are under close scrutiny. Regarding a society's (ideological) preparations for conflict, the term militarisation is often used, reflecting the institutionalised notion of the military in many (Western) countries. Enloe depicts this process as the following:

> Militarisation is a step-by-step process by which a person or a thing comes to be gradually controlled by the military or comes to depend on it for its well being on militaristic ideas. The more militarisation transforms an individual or society, the more that individual or society comes to imagine military needs and militaristic presumptions to be not only normal but valuable (Enloe 2000: 3).

In this light, the question of an adequate terminology of the situation after a war or armed conflict remains. Meintjes et al. chose the term "aftermath", as "post-conflict" did not seem appropriate to them due to the observations that social and economic tensions and violence do not stop with the signing of a peace accord and the halt of the official warfare. They also refuse the term "war-torn societies", as this gives an impression of passive and helpless people who would be waiting for an international community to intervene (Meintjes et al. 2002: 3f.). Taking into account the above understanding of militarised societies, in this book the terms shall be used synonymously with the implication limited to the ending of official warfare. It should be obvious that the time after armed struggle is but a part of the wider cultural and social processes in which militarisms are embedded and did not simply cease to exist or to exert their influences.

In the context of interventions by international institutions such as the UN, one vocabulary is often emerging with regard to women's participation: the rights' based approach. Considering the contestation of the universality of (women's) human rights, this approach may be problematic when trying to implement programmes based on such an understanding as a justification for the participation or integration of women. Yet, as Mackay points out, this approach enables the facilitators to exclude ideas about personal morality or individual views on "'right' or 'wrong'" from the project. Instead, she emphasises they can convey the obligations of all staff to observe and implement the rights (Mackay 2004: 103).

Current discourses and literature

> While the term "Gender" gradually began to enter the literature, the legacy of the "add women and stir" approach lingered until very recently (Wharton 2005: 4).

Wharton points to a problem found in academic literature but also in the field of development practice. While the term gender is used, and in many aid agencies' its use is obligatory, it is often limited to a requirement of (numerically) including women in the analysis or programming. Relating to the current discourse on war, the interrelations of women and armed conflict or small arms is being investigated from various scientific perspectives[1]. Many are aiming at understanding how identities, identity formation or aspects of it, such as gender, are affected by violence. As Jacobs et al. point out, much of this discourse is inspired by a theoretical backup based on feminism. Due to the intricate (conceptual and historical) relationships of women's peace movements and feminist discourse, for a long time the analyses shied at the sphere of women supporting or participating in violence (Jacobs et al. 2000: 12f.). These notions may still be at work when concepts of gender are introduced and claims like the following are made: "Evidence suggests that war is more likely in societies with greater gender inequality" (Tickner 1999: 11; Caprioli 2000)[2]. While direct causal connections between the two phenomena may be doubted (Bilgin 2004), such challenging statements certainly hint to the need of deeper analyses of interrelationships and their effects on people's identity formation processes and the specific role of gender in this context. In this respect Gedalof cautions on the scope of deconstruction as part of postmodernist and poststructuralist (feminist) discourse. In her perspective, they are merely deconstructing to later re-construct identities on a different basis, but without leaving the main determining and fundamentally flawed categories of behind (Gedalof 1999: 8f.).

Despite the inclusion of gender into the analysis, so far the focus of the discourses introduced above remains on women. At the same time, a programmatic tool such as gender mainstreaming is employed in policy and development work, emphasising the interrelationships of genders. While this

---

1 See, amongst others, Farr (2003a); Green (1999); Jacobs et al. (2000); Kelly (2000); Mazurana et al. (2002); Mazurana et al. (2005a); Skjelsbaek and Smith (2001).

2 See also Caprioli (2004); Caprioli and Boyer (2001).

women-centred approach has its limitations, some authors have started to investigate the changing relationships of men and violence in specific circumstances, such as that in Croatia (Zarkov 2001), South Africa (Morrell 2001), within disarmament programmes (Myrttinen 2003) or from a politico-theoretical perspective[1]. A combining and complementary approach has not yet entered the discourse to a substantial extent so that the intended effect gender as an analytical tool should have could be incorporated.

Additionally to the development of the theoretical debate on the inclusion of gender into broader research and policy areas, attention was drawn to the changing kinds of warfare after the end of the Cold War. The academic literature shifted to explaining civil wars, often with an "ethnic" component perceived in their causes. With the shift to internal warfare and the mass proliferation of Small Arms and Light Weapons (SALW) and mines, Volman observed the continuous militarisation of African societies already in 1998, attributing it to easy access to and cheap price of weapons and the continuous conflicts many countries have been experiencing (Volman 1998). Taken together, these changes have a vast effect on the technology and tactics employed in the wars, especially on the civilian population. While no exact numbers are available, estimates reveal that in Word War I it was 10% of the so-called "casualties" who were civilian. With World War II, this number rose to 50% and again increased to 90% for the wars fought in the 1990's (Turpin 1998: 4). Therefore, characteristics of wars changed parallel to an increasing proliferation of SALW in many societies. With these developments in the background, attention has been shifting in some cases from the causes of war to their impact on societies and specific groups of people. In the West African context, the issue of very young combatants in long-lasting civil wars has caught the eyes of researchers and campaigns[2], drawing attention to the devastating consequences of small-arms proliferation.

While the long-held assumptions of predominantly male participation in wars has to be rethought with child combatants as well (see McKay and Mazurana 2004), a growing number of literature is taking up topics in this sphere, from different scientific or professional backgrounds, but so far it is still mostly women writing. The perspectives vary, with some focussing on

---

1 See, amongst others, DeKeseredy and Schwartz (2005); Higate and Hopton (2005); Kegan Gardiner (2005); Nagel (2005).

2 For example: <www.warchild.org>; <www.child-soldiers.org>; <www.hrw.org/campaignes/crp>; <www.amnesty.org/childsoldiers>.

more "technical" aspects of adjusting United Nation's peacekeeping measures to the "needs" of women or including them into the programmes[1], or with special attention to Demobilisation projects[2]. Many of the researchers also work as consultants for the respective organisations, on the one hand introducing a more practice-oriented approach into the research and, on the other hand, potentially giving a different kind of input into the policies later used by international organisations. As such, the present work is drawing on many different kinds of resources with a call for interdisciplinary approaches inherent in them.

Outline

With the main question being whether and how organisations aim to influence potential war-related changes of gender roles with women in a post-conflict setting, the questions introduced above shall be examined more closely in three separate steps. Consequently, the thesis shall be divided into three main parts.

In the following, the second chapter of this book, the theoretical groundwork shall be laid for the successive case study. Drawing on ideas of the interrelationships between gender and identity formation as well as concepts of society, women and conflict, the way war can influence roles in society and especially the roles and identification processes of women shall be examined. First the diverse influences of the war on every-day life, duties and roles during combat shall be the focus, with a later emphasis on the way women face the aftermath of a conflict. In this latter part, the ideas of war empowering women shall be discussed as well as the question whether it is possible for outside influences to support these potential changes or challenges after the war.

While this chapter presents a theoretical approach, some references shall be made to the specific case of Sierra Leone, in preparation for the following case study.

The third chapter will give a closer analysis of the way gender issues were included in the Sierra Leonean DDR programme. For this purpose, the idea of gender mainstreaming and its impacts on the UN system shall be in-

1 See Beilstein (1998); Eifler (2000); Mackay (2004); Olsson (1999); Puechguirbal (2003a/b).

2 See Farr (2002); Mazurana et al. (2002); Watteville (2002); Women's Commission (2002).

troduced. The UN serves as a reference point due to the fact that, in this context it is the major funding and fund-channelling agency. It therefore exerts a large influence on all other organisations, setting implementation standards, leading the discourse and even potentially policy-relevant research on the subject. Due to the limited scope of this book, only a few selected UN organisations shall be considered, all specialised on issues relating to Demobilisation policies or implementation.

In a second step, the DDR process shall be examined more closely with the emphasis on the ways it was addressing combatants and how this especially affected women combatants. As a point of reference, some discussion of the Demobilisation process in neighbouring Liberia is included. The Liberian programme and many of its staff have been transferred from Sierra Leone and were expected to implement the "lessons learnt". Taken together, the analysis of the two DDR processes can give an impression on how persistent ideas of women and of gender mainstreaming processes are within the UN and related organisations.

Having now looked at the theoretical and organisational perspectives on women involved in combat, the fourth chapter shall draw all these together and add the perspective of Sierra Leonean women who have participated in the war in various roles and who were or are still involved in projects linked to Demobilisation. This chapter is based on a representative selection of interviews conducted during fieldwork mainly in the Eastern part of Sierra Leone, a region of the country reckoned to have experienced the longest and most intense warfare. In a first step, the choices women took with regard to the immediate Demobilisation programme shall be examined. In a second step, the way these choices impacted on their lives shall receive attention, reflecting on the involved organisations and their target-group definitions. The subsequent reactions of these women reveal the organisations' influence on perceived roles and processes of identification.

While not wanting to suggest that the interactions between organisations, their programmes and the women in question are one-dimensional or mono-causal, the present book can only capture the above-mentioned interrelationships as part of the multi-dimensional interdependencies of policies, organisations and the people engaging with them.

The remainder of the introduction prepares the grounds for the later analysis. This includes some reflection on fieldwork and interviews to introduce the circumstances of the data collection. Accompanying this is a short overview of Sierra Leone and the recent civil war. An overall history including colonial legacy and recent warfare would be misplaced in the present context as the thesis does not set out to explain war or women's individual or group experiences in the recent conflict.

1.2 Fieldwork and interviews

> The ethnographic reconstruction of violence must write from and towards a ground that few existing moralities can account for. Writing violence becomes the exploration of moralities that have not yet arrived but are busy being born from amoral acts (Feldman 1995: 246).

Drawing on the "writing culture" concept and transferring it into "writing violence"[1], Feldman warns of the moral implications describing war and classifying and therefore evaluating and judging violence. In the many attributes the Sierra Leonean civil war received, trying to convey the horrors and suffering inflicted upon people, a clear moral stance is obvious. But how is one to remain "scientific" in the face of such ferociousness no words are fit to describe. Trying to "factualise and enumerate the horror" was a common Western response, a Sierra Leonean politician pointed out. Indeed this strategy may provide some personal protection, distancing a researcher from moral or emotional involvement. Yet, in the light of advancement of discourse and theory, the strive for a scientific distance has been challenged, including a place for the political and, as Caplan claims, especially in feminist anthropological research (1992: 73).

Fieldwork in the post-conflict setting of Sierra Leone

A variety of (mainly female) authors analyse the experiences of women during war and the consequences on their lives. All of them are dealing with observations of the war. Due to the nature of the present topic, experiences of the war themselves were not central to the research with the processes after its ending being more relevant. Only in retrospective did personal encounters become relevant. Nevertheless, these accounts and the emotions

1 For an overview of anthropological engagement with violence see Scheper-Hughes and Bourgois (2004).

conveyed in them were more taxing in the long run than expected during the initial time spent together.

As a consequence, the book endeavours to walk the fine line between the broader picture of war in Sierra Leone and the personal impressions of the gruesome face of war, related to me by the personal experiences of the women who shared them. Therefore, the present study does not aim to portray the whole war and post-war conditions but a very specific excerpt of a broad variety of possible and actual processes taking place in Sierra Leone today.

The research for this work was conducted with the support of the United Nations Development Fund for Women (UNIFEM) from April to August 2004. This connection provided me with an entry point to the "field", in order to gain insights and learn about mechanisms of the Sierra Leone UN system with regard to their approach towards women and gender mainstreaming, by participating in a diverse range of projects, workshops or public events and thereby experiencing the impacts of hierarchies or the differences of internal and external discourse.

It opened up communication, infrastructure and bureaucracy to travel and do research in the East, North and South of Sierra Leone[1], which would have otherwise taken much longer to organise. In many of the rural parts of the country, two years after the civil war's official end, infrastructural developments were yet to commence and many provisions were not accessible for individuals outside this system. Besides easing travel and therefore research options, the UN link also enabled visits to Liberia[2] which was at that time hard to access for private persons. As a civilian connected to the UN mission in Liberia, I had to adhere to security requirements, sometimes restricting my movements physically and temporarily, more than in neighbouring Sierra Leone.

This infrastructural connection does not imply a focus on the programmes UNIFEM was carrying out or involved in. In fact, at the time of the research, the Fund was neither involved in the DDR programme nor in related activities.

---

1 The research took place mainly in Kono and Kailahun Districts in the Eastern Province, shorter time was also spent in Kambia and Pujehun Districts.

2 Liberia and its local DDR process shall only serve as a reference for the further development of DDR concepts; see chapter 3.2.

Working along my research objectives, I first aimed at gaining organisational insights about the Sierra Leonean DDR. With those infrastructural ties to the UN, I was automatically enabled to enter the field of research. For example, I could directly access the personnel locally involved in the different UN programmes, both on the civilian and military side. With the latter, the military observers (MilObs), stationed around the country instead of remaining in the capital like most of the high-ranking civilian staff, became an important contact point for local UN activities and reflections on long-term peacekeeping and Demobilisation strategies.

Related to these were organisational questions on how institutions were dealing with aspects of gender mainstreaming and affirmative action for women on a policy as well as their practical implementation. Therefore I first concentrated on international and national players, which, due to funding mechanisms, were at the more influential end of the Sierra Leonean civil society. The national and local NGOs opened up new perspectives on Demobilisation work, as personal experiences of the conflict and ties to war participants and individuals' fates were more obvious and relevant within the local settings. At the same time, perspectives on political and technical terms around Demobilisation varied and were related to the regional war history and reflected upon with reference to local concepts of "tradition". These deliberations would potentially oppose the mainstreaming ideals introduced from the outside.

In a second phase I talked to those Sierra Leoneans whom the projects were aiming to reach. Working with women and men who had faced DDR processes with their individual backgrounds, often shaped by ghastly experiences during the war, was awe-inspiring and very moving. At the same time, these conversations gave more reason for optimism and the impression of potential recovery than the institutional perspectives. During this phase "ex-combatants", "war participants", "war victims", "wives of combatants", "abductees", "bush wives", "community youths and leaders" or "local social workers"[1] shared their experiences, attitudes and observations. Many challenged my impressions and thereby furthered my understanding of the research topics.

Despite selective benefits, the connection to the UN posed difficulties as well. Sometimes it gave my person or my presence an official and political

---

1 These are some of the self-assigned titles of interviewees.

character, not in all cases desirable or advantageous (Ferme 2001: 11f.; Hauser-Schäublin 2002). The timing of my fieldwork influenced people's placement of my person and project; yet, it is also vital to understand the potential topics people wanted to talk about. After the war and as a preparation for the reintegration of ex-combatants as well as refugees or returning displaced people, large "sensitisation" programmes were broadcasted on radio or posters to encourage forgiveness and acceptance of the perpetrators of violence and injustice. President Ahmad Tejan Kabbah played a major role in this campaign and people refer to him: "Pa Kabbah told us to forgive the rebels" (*CVT*)[1]. Also, the Truth and Reconciliation Commission (TRC) with its country-wide statement collection and hearings in the district headquarters exerted the message that the people were to forgive and forget in the interest of long-term peace building. This officially induced perspective influenced especially some interviews with office holders such as chiefs or local NGO representatives. The presence of the Special Court, which was in session but still conducted investigations during my fieldwork, also created anxieties. Many people were not sufficiently informed and feared to be prosecuted for war-related actions after the protagonists of the war had been sentenced. This concern was more relevant with women who tended to be less familiar with national or political news than men, as these had more access to radios, the principle channel of information in "upcountry" Sierra Leone.

My mere presence was therefore, even in a rural setting, immediately connected to the UN or one of the above-mentioned institutions. The colour of my skin indicated a hierarchical position within this framework I did not (want to) hold. As some people, especially officials like chiefs or *Sande* leaders had previous experiences with so-called "project finding missions", during first meetings I was often placed into that environment.

Heeding the above-mentioned discourses, exemplified by Feldman (1995) and Caplan (1992), fieldwork in a post-conflict setting such as Sierra Leone became more easily accessible, as the politics of my own person could and had to be included. This was not necessarily only done in an obstructive way, but formed a framework for the research. In certain contexts it would not even have been possible to exclude the personal, the body politics.

---

1 Within this book, the referencing to interviews shall be done in (*italics*). For a detailed list of the interviews cited in this work, see Appendix 7.1.

This did not protect me from the impressions of the civil war, which was characterised by indiscriminate violence. It broke long-standing rules, defiled cherished traditions, sullied human respect and tore apart the very fabric of society (TRC report 2004: Vol. 2: Chap. 2: Clause 21)[1].

It was certainly supportive to be able to put shock, grief, anger or frustration into a (political) framework.

Interviews

> We cannot tell you everything that happened to us during the war. But there was a lot. The memory is still within us (*CASTC*).

Both Ferme (2001) and Shaw (2005) emphasise the great importance of secrecy as opposed to open talking about the general past and specifically the experience of violence in *Mende* and *Temne* traditions respectively. Shaw points out that the official policies of forgetting met concepts of social healing that discouraged open talks about specific crimes or incidents of the past war. Such talk is considered to give life to the past and could therefore reinvoke the violence (2005: 9). History and memory are therefore guided by "the underneath" (Ferme 2001), which in turn influences the way people relate to each other, to social institutions and to processes of (social) healing:

> Among the *Temne*, as well as many other Sierra Leonean and Liberian peoples [...] secrecy pervades social life and social relationships, particularly power relationships. For members of the male and female cult associations, for chiefs and subchiefs, for certain occupational specialists, and for men and women simply as men and women, secret knowledge is used as a basic organising principle by which people define themselves as members of particular groups and as sharing in the power controlled by these groups (Shaw 1992: 44).

Although many counterparts hinted to the important role *Poro* and *Sande* were playing during the war and in the post-conflict stabilisation of social order and sometimes even in the reintegration of (child) ex-combatants[2], I hesitated to enquire more deeply. Nevertheless, these circumstances of se-

1 See also TRC report (2004: Vol. 3A: Chap: 4, p.: 498ff.).
2 See chapters 2.4 and 3.2.

crecy and the inherent presence of the secret societies in the rural settings generally cautioned me not to inquire too forthrightly.

Bearing in mind the above and a comment by Nordstrom, "The most silenced stories at wars' epicentres are generally the most authentic" (cited in Feldman 1995: 249), I did not aim at talking about intimate wartime experiences, unless my interview or discussion partners wished to do so. Yet surprisingly, upon the background of secrecy, individual women talked about rape and related experiences with little reservations. Local NGO staff often indicated that the tremendous and public perpetration of sexual violence and the post-war investigations on human rights' violations by the TRC and related organisations established conversation on certain topics. These processes certainly had repercussions on first meetings and interviews I conducted with some people, supposing me to want to hear similar war narratives, all centred around issues the international human rights discourse is giving voice for. Yet, as Shaw pointed out above, these accounts must be put into perspective vis-à-vis the prevailing notions of secrecy and relations towards outsiders or "strangers" (Richards and Archibald 2002; Richards et al. 2003; Shaw 2002, 2005).

The very precarious subjects of the research made it advisable to choose a flexible and adaptable strategy, leading to my use of semi-structured interviews. This way I could adjust to my counterpart's reactions without major challenges and therefore I was able to adapt individually to how detailed or intimate the topics could be. With a private, or at least non-public, but familiar location, many interviews turned into informal conversations with a lot of new perspectives introduced by my counterparts. These would potentially reveal people's every-day priorities and lead to new lines of thought for the research.

Contacts to the women and men I talked to were mostly established through local institutions, either through former reintegration projects of the DDR or people working in the local civil society with a focus on women. Some of them organised group discussions and invited people they knew. As a result of such meetings, personal interviews or new contacts led me to leave the project environment in which the first group of people was usually situated and I could get in touch with women who did not take part in any projects.

Talking to local NGO staff or prominent members of the community such as town chiefs or elders sitting on the local court was often an obligation, especially in rural settings, however, here I received a lot of information of a more official nature, revealing personal ties and institutional structures in the villages or towns. Often, one meeting led to another, with people wanting me to meet a friend or relative who would maybe like to meet me as well. These then were much more personal encounters.

In most of these cases I either took notes during the interviews or immediately afterwards. My knowledge of Krio is limited, nonetheless with a mixture of Krio and English conversations proceeded without major problems. I mostly prioritised an atmosphere of privacy rather than inviting a third person to give a perfect translation.

The interviews I conducted in Freetown or the major cities, with UN or NGO staff differ a great deal from those described above. Language issues did not occur as English and only rarely a mix of English and Krio were used. The topics were more programme- or organisation-centred, less personal or emotional, as a consequence recording was more often an option. With sensitive topics relating to either personal impressions of the programme or the organisations involved, in some cases requests for anonymity prohibited recording.

The interviews cited in this work are a selection of the many I conducted. Some were of a more personal, others only of official concerns so I decided to omit them. Others contained such gruesome war experiences that it seemed inappropriate to include these. The choice I use here focuses on those typical interviews concerning the interaction of women and men combatants or other war participants with the organisations and programmes that are the focus of this book.

1.3 The local context

Sierra Leone is located at the heart of the Upper Guinea Coast[1]. The majority of the rural population is dependent on subsistence rice farming, which is largely conducted with slash and burn cultivation techniques adapting to the tropical weather cycle of rainy (April to October) and dry seasons. These not only influence agricultural but also economic and social activities (Schäfer 1995: 128). Rice is both cultivated in upland and swamp varieties and forms

1 For a map of Sierra Leone see Appendix 7.2.

a vital part in the nutritional and symbolic life of many communities. Traditionally, many activities were also influenced and guided by secret societies, which contribute to shared political, cultural and ethnic identities, but also work across these lines to integrate the different people under the umbrella of male and female sodalities. The major ethnic groups in Sierra Leone are the *Temne* in the North and Northwest and the *Mende* in the South and Southeast of the country, with the latter being subdivided into the *Kpa-*, *Ko-* and *Sewa-Mende* based on dialect groups (Schäfer 1995: 128). The most prominent of the smaller ethnic groups are the *Sherbro* in the Southwest, the *Kissi* in the South and the *Kono* in the Northeast of Sierra Leone. *Koranko* and *Limba* settle in the North of the country. *Fula* and *Mandingo* are, linked to their origins as traders, distributed all over the country. The *Krio* also play an important, but diminishing role in Sierra Leone society (Cartwright 1970: 50ff.). They are descendents of freed slaves brought to the Western peninsula from the late 18th century onwards.[1]
The West African slave trade not only influenced the coastal areas of Sierra Leone, but also in the country's interior in diverse and multiple ways. Effects of these past events can still be felt in today's society and its practices (Shaw 2002). While people were involved as traders, they were also traded as slaves themselves. Within some ethnic groups, domestic slavery was common and only abolished in the 20th century by the colonial administration. Ferme even claims that some social relations were sometimes hard to distinguish from domestic slavery and even today cannot be understood without the history and concepts of slave trade. She views *Mende* practices of fostering, adoption and marriage in this light (Ferme 2001: 82). According to the author, gender relations are immersed into these long-term effects of slavery and introduce historically shaped forms of dependencies into the domestic and family sphere (Ferme 2001: 18).

The British colonial administration of the 19th century elaborated a hierarchical system of paramount, village and section chiefs, which is still in place, part of the current constitution and often embodies the only effective representation of the state, especially in remote areas of the country. Under the British colonial rule, these chiefly families developed into what Kilson termed "tradition-modern elites" as over time they were able to incorporate

1 For further literature on the Krio see Dixon-Fyle and Cole (2006); Knörr (1995); Wyse (1989).

traditional elements of power and landownership with modern statesmanship, educational and professional achievements (1966: 65).

Chieftaincy is intertwined with and checked by *Poro* and *Sande*, therefore in many groups the position of the chief excludes a leading position in secret society. Nevertheless, both spheres are dominated by local land-controlling lineages, in some places called Ruling Houses. Status and position within some *Mende* and *Sherbro* lineages were more important than gender when it came to allocation or election of posts (Schäfer 1995: 129). As such, historically women did play important political roles in the South of Sierra Leone, as chiefs or other high offices (Hoffer 1972).

Women in Sierra Leone

Considering the many different groups living in Sierra Leone, the situation of women must be differentiated along multiple lines. As many other factors additionally influence people's lives, it is impossible to portray them in a short overview. Therefore the focus here shall lie on the legal situation of women in Sierra Leone, giving an impression of the larger framework of their positions in society.

One major dividing element in the country is the differentiation between the Western Area with Freetown and the "Provinces"[1]. Legally, the population of the latter are governed by Customary Law, un-codified collections of "traditional" laws implemented by local courts in a society, which Aning describes as "very conservative and patriarchal […] where women have traditionally taken a secondary position to men" (1998: 2). As a consequence, women married under this law are legally regarded as "chattel" (Molloy 2004: 18; TRC report 2004: Vol. 3B: Chap. 3: Clause 64), as a Justice of the Peace pointed out regarding women's rights: "I don't understand what you want. The law is the law. And the law says you [a woman] are like a table in my house. So I can treat you like that. This is what the law says" (*Mr. Kalon*).

With about 65% of the population, mainly in the northern part of Sierra Leone, being Muslims, people in these areas are also governed by Islamic Law, which for example grants women the role of a minor in relation to their

1 Due to geography, colonial history and infrastructure, the Western Area with the capital is perceived as quite separate from the rest of the country, which is referred to as "the Provinces".

fathers or husbands and limits their property and inheritance rights as well as the accessibility of divorce or formal legal protection (Bouta et al. 2005: 79). The legal system of the Western Area is based on British Common Law of the 19th century[1], again not recognising women as equal or full citizens. At the same time, Sierra Leone is signatory to international human rights and women's rights conventions such as CEDAW, the International Convention on Economic, Cultural and Social Rights (ICECSR), the International Convention on Civil and Political Rights (ICCPR), the African Charter on Human and People's Rights and the Convention of the Rights of the Child (CRC), with all of them acknowledged in the constitution[2]. For example, the application of personal law based on religious values, like in the case of Islam, violates directly the provisions of CEDAW on non-discrimination, even on the background of the convention valuing cultural and religious particularities in communities (Merry 2005: 229).

The overall result in the case of Sierra Leone is a contradictory legal system which is highly discriminative against women (Richards et al. 2004: 6, 40). The constitution explicitly states the overruling powers of Customary Law with regard to personal law, including marriage, property or inheritance rights. Yet, it is these spheres that determine women's ever-day lives to a large extent. The inaccessibility of the formal legal system, with most disputes settled locally by chiefs or Justices of the Peace, leads to women's further subjugation to established power relations and male-defined family necessities (*Kariatu*). According to Turshen, this has the greatest effect on women's lives and poses the biggest challenge for potential change in the aftermath of a conflict (2001: 78).

Another important dimension for every-day life is whether women live in a rural or urban environment. As the vast majority lives in rural settings, these shall be considered in the following introduction. In remote areas, women marry at an average age of 15.5 years, after being initiated into the *Sande*, or locally termed *Bundu* secret society (Richards et al. 2004: 5). Institutions determining marriage are lineage exogamy, virilocality, polygyny and to some extent the levirate, with a substantial bride price being paid to the *Sande* initiators and the bride's family (Schäfer 1995: 134). Due to the

1 For example, the law referred to in cases of rape is the British "Offence against Persons Act" of 1861 (Bouta et al. 2005: 79).

2 For further details on the conventions and their implications for Sierra Leone see TRC report (2004: Vol. 3B: Chap. 3: Clause 154ff.).

limited ability of young men to provide such a payment, age-differences within a marriage are high, with the husband often already being married to several wives, undermining the bride's negotiating powers vis-à-vis himself and the senior wives (Richards et al. 2004: 14). In the following life cycle, the status of women depends on the position of her husband's family, her age, the number of her children and her seniority regarding her co-wives. In rural areas, women are providing most of the labour for subsistence farming and are therefore the main caretakers for their families regarding day-to-day needs.

Throughout a woman's life, *Sande*[1] rules and leading members exert a large amount of control due to "secret knowledge" on fertility and child birth and the power to implement social regulations, fines or other punishments. This is part of a larger network controlling especially young women due to their productive and reproductive capacities, first exploited by their family of origin, later by their husband's family, and starting from the beginning of their initiation also by leaders of the local *Sande* society. This control network, intertwined with values and beliefs, is able to keep women submissive to any figure of authority (Fuest 1999: 81ff.).

Considering the above factors, local women's organisations and parts of the international community are calling for major changes regarding the situation of women in Sierra Leone. The latter use indicators like low literacy rate, high maternal mortality and the low rate of women in political decision making positions to point out the "marginalisation and disempowerment" of women in the country (Wakhweya et al. 2002: 17). A national consultative meeting on this topic called for wide changes in law and administration as well as in public life, to assure gender equality and equity. The recommendations assert that women are exposed to gross discrimination and violations of their (human) rights if these rights should be considered overpowering local or customary law. Currently, Sierra Leone's constitution does not clarify the interrelations of different laws and conventions. Instead, it accepts them on a par. (National Consultation 2001: 5). The TRC report finds even more explicit words:

1 For a detailed account on *Sande* among the *Mende* of Sierra Leone see Schäfer (1990).

> Women and girls in Sierra Leone continue to suffer historic structural inequality on account of their gender. Gender inequality is entrenched in all spheres of social, political and economic life by discriminatory laws, customs, traditions and practices (2004: Vol. 2: Cap: 3: Clause 319).

On this issue, the TRC gave the imperative recommendation to repeal the contradicting parts of the constitution and secure women's equal rights, as "discrimination on the basis of gender have no place in a modern democratic society based on equality and respect for human dignity" (2004: Vol. 2: Cap: 3: Clause 342–344).

Additionally, it called on parliament to abolish those parts of the customary law that are discriminating against women, focussing on inheritance, land ownership, marriage, divorce and administration of estates (2004: Vol. 2: Cap: 3: Clause 345). While the TRC report acknowledges the importance and value of customary law (Clause 107) or other local institutions, such as *Bundu* (Clause 372), it decidedly demands the customary laws' codification and simultaneous harmonisation with international conventions on the rights of women and children (Clause 109–111). These matters, according to the report, should be taken care of in a law reform commission, which is generally to review the constitution (Clause 192–196).

While these recommendations may reflect the official discourse on the situation of women in Sierra Leone, the implementation of the recommendations is at the disposal of the government and the many local and social institutions involved in bringing about change.

History of the war and present context

History shows that in the past Sierra Leoneans successfully deployed a range of strategies – including secrecy – to live in the proximity of death. Secrecy does not offer the teleological certainty of realisable political projects. However, Sierra Leoneans have lived this social instability before, and they have sometimes turned it into a creative, though violent, opportunity to refashion themselves vis-à-vis their own institutions (Ferme 2001: 228).

The international media largely ignored the civil war in Sierra Leone. Except for the topic of "blood diamonds", finding its international ramification in the Kimberley Process[1], and the issue of child combatants, large-scale vio-

1 See, amongst others, AMCO (2002); Campbell (2002); Gberie (2004); Wright (2004).

lence inflicted on the civilian population escaped international attention (Humphreys and Weinstein 2005). Some commentators refer to it as one of "Africa's most brutal civil wars" (Aning 1998: 21).

In the light of the war itself and considering the gruesome and ghastly atrocities perpetrated in its name, different authors proposed varying explanations of its cause and course: from the problem of the youth and young excluded intellectuals (Bangura 1997; Richards 1996), to diamonds, other natural resources as well as corruption and patrimonial power relations (Abdullah 1997; Reno 2001). These are but some of the attempts to explain a vast potential for civil war which then was used by political and military entrepreneurs, from some author's perspective institutionalised in the rebel group "Revolutionary United Front of Sierra Leone" (Gberie 2005; Keen 2005; Richards 2002). The TRC report centres its findings on war causes on the "endemic greed, corruption and nepotism that deprived the nation of its dignity and reduced most people into a state of poverty" (2004: Vol. 2: Chap. 3: Clause 34; also see Vol. 2: Chap. 2: Clause 39–74). These investigations into the war represent different and sometimes contradictory explanations of the foundation and outbreak of the war, with all of them using different emphases when investigating its local causes. While authors such as Elwert (1999) try to explain the logic or reason behind wars and their political economy[1], others deliberately refuse to try and search for reason in view of the bloodshed (Nordstrom 1995: 137; Robben and Nordstrom 1995).

While a full description of the war is beyond the scope of this work, a few details shall be noted to introduce key players, their factions and strategies, as far as they are relevant to the thesis.

The recent history of Sierra Leone can be divided into four phases of armed conflict. The impetus towards conflict was growing from the end of colonial rule in 1961 through the slow disintegration into "patrimonial and predatory rule" with changing civilian and military governments (Sawyer 2004: 442). This resulted in widespread dissatisfaction amongst the population. The actual war began when an armed group called "Revolutionary United Front of Sierra Leone" (RUF/SL) entered the country from the Liberian border zone in 1991. The initial invasion was composed primarily of Liberian fighters from Charles Taylor's NPFL. Though the stated aim of the

1 In German, Elwert coined the term "Gewaltunternehmer", emphasising the political economy of warlords' strategies and activities.

force was to topple the APC government in Freetown their activities were confined to the South and East of the country.

The initial successes of the RUF/SL insurgence could be correlated with the failure of the government to protect and defend its citizens. Accordingly, it was overthrown by a military coup in 1992, resulting in the government of the "National Provisional Ruling Council" (NPRC). Initially the NPRC prosecuted the war successfully, driving the RUF fighters back towards the Liberian border. However in the second phase of the war, beginning in 1994, the RUF/SL changed tactics. Their switch to guerrilla warfare could not be opposed effectively by the NPRC government. The change to bush-based fighting was an impetus for further kidnapping of women and girls into sexual and domestic servitude (*Richard Conibere*). Doubting the Sierra Leone Army's potential to deal with the RUF/SL, the NPRC hired the South African private security firm "Executive Outcomes", paying them with diamond concessions (Humphreys and Weinstein 2005: 11).

The civilian population in the south and east of the country had been most affected by the insurgency and began to locally organise defence groups, which should protect villages and towns against RUF/SL but also "sobels"[1]. They were based on and derived their structures and power from the presumed "traditional" hunters connected to the *Poro* secret societies. Accordingly, their organisational structures and names ran along ethnic lines and they fought predominantly in their respective areas of settlement. Among the different groups, Alie identifies the *Tamaboros* (in Koinadugu District), the *Donsos* (in Kono District) and *Kamajors* (in the East and South of Sierra Leone) as the earliest defence groups (2005: 55). All of them were later joined under the umbrella of the "Civil Defence Force" (CDF), once the NPRC passed the power on to the elected government of President Kabbah in 1996 (Muana 1997).

A third phase of the civil war can be identified when only one year later the Kabbah-government was overthrown by another military coup during a resurgence of RUF/SL violence, this time a breakaway from the regular army. The young officers of the "Armed Forces Revolutionary Council" (AFRC) allied themselves with the RUF/SL and invited them to join their government in Freetown. In early 1998 Nigerian-lead ECOMOG troops ex-

1 This word emerged on the background of the Sierra Leonean war meaning "soldier by day, rebel by night" (Richards 1996: 7), indicating the dire states of equipment and provision as well as training and discipline of the national army.

pelled this military government to restore the previous civilian one in the capital. Meanwhile the war continued in other parts of the country, uninterrupted by the events in the capital.

By this time the *Kamajor* (a *Mende*-based CDF group) had been armed by the government and effectively protected the South of the country. Thus the remnants of the AFRC with affiliated RUF/SL-members regrouped and fled to the North, executing a "massive campaign of banditry and terror". In what was arguably the "culmination of the war" (*Richard Conibere*), forces loyal to the AFRC returned to attack Freetown at the beginning of 1999. The West African peace forces pushed them back.

The fourth and final phase, after the signing of the Lomé peace accord, was characterised by moves towards peace and resurgent violence. The Lomé agreement granted amnesty to combatants, preparing for elections, a United Nations Mission (UNAMSIL), a Truth and Reconciliation Commission and stating the basics for the Disarmament, Demobilisation and Reintegration programme. Taking part in the elections, the RUF/SL failed to win a single seat in parliament. This rekindled the armed conflict and disrupted the disarmament process substantially (Sawyer 2004: 449). Some AFRC remnants formed the "West Side Boys" and stayed in the hills outside Freetown, terrorising the peninsula. Despite the signatures on the peace agreement and the increased deployment of the UN peacekeeping forces, sporadic fighting continued until 2002, when President Kabbah announced the final end of the civil war (PHR 2002: 21).

Throughout the war, conflicts and developments in neighbouring countries would be fuelling the fighting in Sierra Leone, with large amounts of refugees and combatants crossing the borders in all directions (Sawyer 2004: 446). Therefore, the prospects for a lasting peace continue to be insecure "due in part to the combustible [Mano River] basin-wide environment in which Sierra Leone is situated […] and the nature of the governance relations reconstituted" (Sawyer 2004: 450).

Currently, the withdrawing of the UNAMSIL peacekeeping troops on 31st December 2005, only leaving behind the political advisory office UNIOSIL, and the simultaneous increase in local tensions, with the reinstallation of those people who had been in powerful political (and economic) positions before and partly during the war adds to the population's lack of confidence in a peaceful future: "If you imagine that UNAMSIL was spread over the country like a beautiful carpet, well now the time has come to roll that carpet back, and what you might find underneath may not be very good" (SRSG Mwakawago, quoted in IRIN 2005).

As it is impossible to summarise the numerous, disparate and brutal atrocities, war crimes and war-related sufferings, there can only be estimates of the true effects the war has and continues to have on the people involved in and affected by it. With the horrific violations in mind, reciting or calculating numbers in some instances even seems inappropriate as figures of dead, wounded or amputated people can only give an indication of the gross human suffering and the horrors individual Sierra Leoneans lived through. Long-term physical, psychological and social consequences of the war are beyond imagination.

Unlike the conflicts in neighbouring Guinea and Liberia, Sierra Leone has not experienced explicitly ethnically or religiously inspired violence (Foray 2000: 99). Nonetheless, widespread violence and terror inflicted on the civilian population deliberately targeted "people's sense of family and community, shattering the foundations of their cultural and human existence" (Robben and Nordstrom 1995: 18). Relatives, friends and neighbours have perpetrated atrocities so that grave dividing lines run through the population.

Women in the war

Like in many wars, women were exposed to systematic rape and other kinds of sexual torture (HRW 2003; PHR 2002; TRC report 2004: Vol. 3B: Chap. 3). Cultural taboos were attacked and broken by not sparing suckling mothers from rape or splitting open pregnant women to determine the sex of the unborn child, both being regarded as especially gruesome[1]. Such activities are perceived to have "undermined the cultural fabric of values and traditions" holding together society (*Richard Conibere*). In this atmosphere of sexual violence, the very fact of being a woman enabled some to "socially navigate" (Utas 2005a) their way through the war by forming strategic relationships with captors or comrades, ensuring their own survival and often those of their children as well[2].

---

1 On the relevance of traditions or customs in perpetrating violence during war see Thompson and Eade (2004: 233), on symbolic aspect of violence see, amongst others, Bordieu (2001); Cimet (2002).

2 For a comparable case, see Utas' studies on the Liberian war (2005a/b).

However, women were not only the target of violence, many of them also took an active part in it. While it is a fact that women were represented in all factions fighting, the debated question remains to what extent and with which responsibilities. A survey by Humphreys and Weinstein compares the NCDDR number of women in fighting factions of 7.4% with their own finding of an average of 10.9%, yet note that they suspect the total number to be higher (2004: 14). In another report concerning Sierra Leonean disarmament, the authors note that gender-disaggregated data, other than the total number of participants, was not available, hampering the statistical research options on this topic (Miller et al. 2006: 15).

For the RUF/SL, a lot of oral testimonies assert that women could be found in all levels, from combatants and field commanders to RUF/SL leaders and "diplomats". Apparently, the organisation had a whole women's section, the "Women Auxiliary Corps" (TRC report 2004: Vol. 3B: Chap. 3: Clause 393), which was present and working at all levels (Aning 1998: 13). The political wing of the RUF/SL certainly had prominent women amongst their ranks. Nonetheless, they were certainly incorporated due to the fact that they belonged to the tradition-modern elite (Kilson 1966: 65) of the areas controlled. Some of these women also took part in RUF/SL's war council or actively supported the AFRC's regime and warfare in political or diplomatic positions (Mansaray 2000: 144ff.). Richards contests the systematic integration of women into the different organisational divisions of the various factions in the Sierra Leone war. In his perspective, individual women could take positions, but no systematic approach was ever taken to integrate them in higher-level hierarchies. Only on combat level, he asserts the existence of special "combat wives units" (Richards 2002: 262).

As the empirical part of the present work will focus on the Eastern Province of Sierra Leone, with RUF/SL having been the prominent occupiers of the area for a long time, it is this faction that the following considerations shall draw upon. While abduction into RUF/SL was one of the more common ways for women to enter, voluntary or other recruitment mechanisms also took place. On this background the broad military training of women is contested. The impressions from the literature and from the fieldwork are ambiguous, leading to the assumption that this issue was treated differently in every fighting group or unit. Some younger female informants even pointed out that they were trained together with boys, having to fulfil exactly the same training requirements and otherwise being assigned the same chores regarding camp maintenance and the like. Some women had constant access to weapons; others were only given one immediately before an attack. While some women claimed that everyone had to participate in combat, others said that only the "fierce" ones took part.

Accounts of women's responsibilities and experiences during the war therefore vary greatly. In a survey by Mazurana and Carlson on the everyday tasks of female combatants during the Sierra Leonean civil was, the women associated the following (job) descriptions to their regular chores: 72% cooks, 68% porters, 62% assisting sick and wounded, 60% wives, 44% food producers, 40% messengers, 22% spies, 18% communication technicians, 14% workers in alluvial diamond mines for a "captor husband" or commander. These tasks fell outside the fighting responsibilities, for which nearly half of the women who participated in this study had been trained (Mazurana and Carlson 2004: 12).

During combat and outside of it, women lived through many different events of such a variety that they could hardly be amassed and then fit into the stereotypical characterisation of a soldier. Instead, they lead to contradictory, overlapping and complementary roles during war.

2 Women and war

2.1 Identities and gender roles as group phenomena

Feminist scholarship of women and gender

The issue of women, gender, war and violence have received growing attention among academics since the 1990s. Despite the introduction of gender as an analytical tool, the main reference point remains the dichotomy between men and women as part of the many dualisms (Western) theoretical practice and also even some feminist theories employ (Gedalof 1999: 177). Ideas of women and men therefore still feature highly in the discourse of war and its effects on people. If women are the focus of this attention,

> [t]he ensuing narrative either insists upon women's victimhood and their helplessness in the face of suffering and adversity; or it stresses their resourcefulness, their 'inner strength', their stoical struggle to keep their families going, their 'natural' identification with peace (Eade 2004: x).

The analysis of women's experiences as victims or as active agents of peace reflects this dichotomy and is part of a special theoretical perspective. Stereotyping and dichotomisation were still dominating scholars' and practitioners' impressions, which was "damaging to women, particularly to their credibility as actors in matters of international politics and national security, but they are also damaging to peace" (Tickner 1999: 4).

As Gedalof points out with reference to Foucault, (negotiating) power cannot be dichotomised as present or absent but rather as "diffuse and multivocal" (1999: 177). In the present context, women's life realities in war should therefore be mediated between the above-mentioned two extremes of victimhood and active agency by various accesses to powers. These they attain by participating in war and violence in multiple roles and functions as well as suffering from its consequences.

Analysing "women and war", it must be remembered that women are not a homogenous group but differ in many ways, which shape their agency during and after conflict. The analysis should therefore enable these "multiple rather than singular expressions of gender". The differences amongst women and men go beyond class, race or age and are based on cultural and traditional backgrounds, at the same time as being integrated into other, contributing factors of identities (Wharton 2005: 5). These observations directly point to the fact that some forms of femininities and masculinities are socially more valued than others and are therefore positively sanctioned.

Gender relations can clearly not be fully understood by examining only one gender; they are all interdependent and embedded into wider frameworks of power relations taking place in the broader context of society. Changes with one will directly affect the other. Yet, such interrelations are not always considered, as Oyewumi shows in her analysis of the international community's newly attained focus on gender. In her view, organisations and their programmes are promoting the simplification of women's source of power by reducing their roles in societies to wives and housewives, undermining all other roles and therefore also options for women's agency (Oyewumi 2002: 4).

Heeding the above caution, a possible way not to analyse women and women's agency isolated from the wider community, is to look at women's identities as parts of communities' identity discourses. This way it should be possible to highlight the close connection between women's identities and communal identities. How women are employed as "community signifiers" (see Yuval-Davis 1992) also has an effect on the flexibility and negotiability of their individual identities, on gender relations and the power to question the traditional ways of the wider societies.

Women, gender and the formation of collective identities[1]

The intellectual challenge of identity lies in the exercise of adding gender to the arsenal of analytical tools to rethink identity, so that we can deepen our understanding of power and increase our strategic capacity to engage with and challenge its destructive capacity (Mama 2001: 6f.).

1 While discussions on women's identities as part of communal or group identities are mostly featuring in debates on nation and nation building, these can serve as reference for the efforts communities take to restrain women by identity politics on any level of society.

While some researchers are quite critical on whether gender as an analytical tool studying the formation of identities can be applied in all societies (see, amongst others, Okome 2001; Oyewumi 2001, 2002), Mama perceives it as a challenge to be integrated into the discourses on identities and power relationships. At the same time she remains critical of the concept and claims that people in African settings are much more immersed in family or other group concepts than can be captured with a "western" scientific model of "identity", resulting in a segregating, individualistic concept. Similar to Oyewumi, she alleges that the concept of gender is used to reduce and oversimplify interpersonal relationships in society (Mama 2001: 1). However, in contrast to the above-mentioned authors, Mama acknowledges it to be an approved and appropriate analytical tool to examine power relations in society, if the individualising understanding of both identity and gender are incorporated into the analysis.

Trying to bridge this perceived gap between group-based power discourses in society and gender as an individualistic notion, Wharton states that gender should not be limited to characterising an individual, but as influencing all spheres of societal structures. This makes gender identity into a group phenomenon, which is reflected in interaction, social processes and institutions independently from the individual. Wharton points to the fact that gender is being embodied within and reproduced by the institutions of society and should therefore be very much fit to examine the power relations within a group (Wharton 2005: 7).

While no claim should be made that (gendered) roles in society match concepts of identities or are even synonymous, there are relationships and interdependences. If differences in gender shape social interaction and institutions, access to social resources will also be linked to gender, making it relevant to a person's socialisation and agency.

At the same time as conflicting researchers such as Okome, Oyewumi and Mama disagree about the level of gender's influence on an individual's or a community's identity, other authors ascribe gender a larger meaning. Wharton assumes that it "may be among the most influential in shaping the standards people hold for themselves" (2005: 9). Skjelsbaek even terms gender the "master identity", as it determined the "central aspects of our social worlds" (1997: 9). As such, the analytical degree to which gender is relevant to a specific social institution may vary, it is never the less an integral part of the institution and of its ways to discuss and reinforce its rules and regulations (Wharton 2005: 10).

Both identity, and as its integral part, gender are therefore decisive parameters of locating an individual in the power discourses of societies, drawing on Foucault's ideas that society does not have spheres void of power and of power discourses (1978). Following his idea, the power attributed to gender relationships can be enabling and constraining at the same time. As identities are subject to many different changes and conditions that are interrelated, every individual has agency to exert some influence on identities (Gedalof 1999: 174). At the same time Salih, referring to Butler, points out that these agencies could not support an individual to freely upset or break out of the power discourses. She argues that, as a subject immersed in power relationships, the individual has to submit itself to social identity concepts that are imposed onto the individual by society. Instead of opposing these powers, the individual is "passionately attached" to them. This emotional relationship reveals that for a person "it is impossible to evade or transcend the power structures within which [...] [identity]-formation occurs" (Salih 2002: 119).

Discourses of and on identities are therefore collective projects taking place within and amongst groups. They affect the individual person, making it a subject to continuous change and renegotiation of identity as it is constituted at cross sections of diverse roles, expectations and responsibilities of the wider society and its discourses. Yet, as the individual is also part of the group and participates in its activities and negotiations, it has (limited) influence on identity discourses as well, employing its agency within a given framework.

According to Pettman, "gendered identity politics" make specifically women the "markers of community boundaries". This is due to their "dual reproductive role" as mothers and as providers for the family (Pettman 1999: 214f.). Women appear to become not only physical but also cultural reproducers of a community as "women are often the ones given the social role of inter-generational transmitters of cultural traditions, customs, songs, cuisine, and, of course, the mother tongue" (Yuval-Davis 1992: 8)[1].

Henceforth, the role of women as "border guards" of a group enhances the ambiguity regarding their position in the power discourse described

1 See also Knörr and Meier (2000); White (1987).

above. On the one hand they are full members or even regarded as especially valuable due to reproductive capacities. On the other hand specific rules and regulations apply to them as they bear the "burden of representation" of the group (Werbner and Yuval-Davis 1999: 13). According to some authors, this tension or ambiguity results in a specific scrutiny of women in some communities. Concepts of tradition, culture, (family) honour or the integrity of ethnic groups or the nation[1] are being manifested in women's bodies, a process which Nagel identifies as "ethnosexual frontiers" (1999: 102). Such an attitude may then lead to more control over the behaviour and sexuality of female group members, with this control exerted in diverse and multiple ways (Werbner and Yuval-Davis 1999: 16; Nagel 2003).

As gender is part of identity processes on group level, the roles attributed on the basis of gender are very context specific. Therefore, they have the potential to change throughout time as circumstances and meanings shift and give way to new perceptions of roles and identities in a specific group. This process might or might not cut across ethnic, class or similar boundaries (Mazurana and Carlson 2004: 13). War or armed conflict can cause such shifts and changes within and between groups, which then affect gendered roles and self-images, and therefore possibly also identity formation processes. Before such processes can be examined, it should be noted that wars or armed conflicts are not isolated events but are embedded in societies and therefore also in identity formation mechanisms.

2.2 Relationships of society, women and conflict

Before going into details on how women, men and their individual self-perceptions could be affected by violent conflicts, different dimensions of wars' effects on societies shall be shortly introduced to prepare a closer look onto women's specific experiences within the wider society. During this discourse the large diversity of people, individual preconditions and experiences as well as the wars themselves shall remain as a background against which the heterogeneity of people's interactions with conflict can be explained.

1 For case studies, see amongst others, Collier (1997) and Kligman (1998).

Conflict and war embedded in societies

Often wars or violent conflicts are held to be extraordinary, involving the rare and exceptional overthrow of the peaceful rule of law and order. This perspective stems from an angle emphasising peace as the "natural" state of societies. Yet, the line between war and peace can be very thin, especially from a long-term social perspective. Du Nann Winter et al. remind us that war cannot erupt out of nowhere but is part of societies even when they are not currently involved in open warfare (Du Nann Winter et al. 2001). Their approach investigates overt social mobilisation for wars and their endorsement by supportive ideologies, of which one part is structural violence in Galtung's notion (1985), linked to questions of broader power discourses in society.

For the purpose of this book, wars can be understood as "organised purposeful group action, directed against another group" (Ferguson 1990: 26). If war is an enterprise undertaken by a group with specific interests, targeting another group, some ideology or motivation must allow for the mobilisation of resources and people. This is widely referred to as militarism, though the concept is not based or limited to the regular establishment of a national military or army (Lamb 2000: 124ff.). Researchers assert that most societies are militarised by a set of values that "support military activities and enable countries to mobilise for war. Militarism is as important during peace as it is during war" (Du Nann Winter et al. 2001: 139).

Apart from this overt and direct employment of social institutions for the purpose of warfare, Elwert points to a more differentiated and intricate approach of analysing the processes of preparing and creating violence. He introduces the concept of differently embedded differently escalating conflicts. From a situation in which the conflicts in a given society are not embedded to the extent that they could be resolved by commonly acknowledged procedures, avoidance is the usual way of reaction. If this strategy should fail and violence increases, then the conflict can hardly be resolved within embedded structures of organised and acknowledged procedures or official and structured warfare, but results in destruction, exemplified, on a large scale, in genocide (Elwert 2004: 31). The conflict in Sierra Leone can serve as an example of such a process, in which conflict resolution mechanisms of avoidance failed due to long-lasting and continuously increasing disempowerment of the population and rising levels of poverty (see TRC report 2004: Vol. 2: Chap. 2: Clause 21). The limited integration capacity of state institutions, its loss of the legitimate monopoly of violence and its ability to allow for competition in the national power discourse (Zürcher 2004: 105), led to inability of the conflict to stay embedded in the Sierra Leonean society and according to Elwert's concept resulted in a regular war.

These mechanisms should suggest, that the relationships between wars and societies cannot be reduced to destruction but also have integrating and challenging effects that could lead a society into cohesion. However, Christophe cautions on this aspect: violence and destruction should never be underestimated to appear harmless so that a "harmonious" picture of a warring or highly militarised society could be painted (2004: 231).

By accepting war or armed conflict as well as systems of values supporting them as being somewhat part of many societies[1], it can be assumed that societies have established coping strategies to deal with social and emotional effects of militarism, militarisation[2] and the consequences of war. Bracken points out how important the local and "indigenous" coping strategies are to support social and cultural healing processes in a post-conflict setting, as they are more appropriately adapted to perceptions and needs than interpretations from the outside (1998: 57).

Militarisation along gendered lines – militarised gender constructs

Having indicated the intricate relations between wars and societies in general, even during times of peace, the way women are drawn into systems of wars and violence shall now be analysed. This system appears to be dominated by men regarding positions and ranks, decision-making processes and agency (Skjelsbaek 2001: 5). According to Enloe, history neglects women and women's role in the military and wars. Yet, with issues of women and war entering feminist discussions, women's various roles and long-term involvement are being highlighted. These often focus on the "traditional role" of women as providers and caretakers, which make military depend on women as nurses, cooks or free-time companions, even if this is mostly not recognised officially (Enloe 2000: 36). She further claims that women as

1 For an anthropological perspective on war, relating the idea of wars being inherently part of groups and societies, see Orywal et al. (1996).

2 The term militarisation shall not be limited to Lamb's perspective (2000), focussing on military's institutionalised relations to politics and society, but shall include broader ideological aspects of militarism as discussed by Du Nann Winter et al. (2001).

camp followers, long-term companions of troops and war, had been ignored due to certain qualities attributed to them that opposed specific ideas of "traditional femininity" (p. 34), in the sense of reproducing and caring for the families far away from the battle fields. The acceptable areas of women supporting the military were limited to cheering the troops and providing technical and medical infrastructure afar from front lines. Women were therefore supposed to "set the atmosphere" for war by establishing a feeling of collective determination and identity, which had to be protected and fought for by the men (Green 1999: 85ff.). This phenomenon leads Turpin to claim that "war magnifies already existing gender inequalities and women's subordination" which are embedded in peacetime society and later instrumentalised for war purposes (1998: 15).

From the above, it follows that ideas of masculinities and femininities are interrelated and integrated into an ideology preparing society for violent conflict, which is working along established power relations within the society (Moser 2001: 34). This way, questions of gender become part of militarisation processes and shape ideas of who can get involved and how they can be involved in aggression or violence (Farr 2003a: 28). Acceptability of (usually male) aggressive behaviour or the availability of arms belong to this sphere. Domestic violence is an important indicator for societies' norms of violence. Changes of its prevalence and intensity indicate gender relations in the wider society and the way social crises are transferred into the families (Eifler 2004: 259). All these factors influence the ways societies deal with violence of all kinds and at all levels, with interpersonal violence being just as much part of this phenomenon as political, economic or social violence are.

Accordingly, concepts relating to violence and the appropriate behaviour during conflict are part of identity constructs along gendered lines, or in other words, part of gender roles as well. From this condition it follows that women are part of the system surrounding and supporting war, even if they are not directly contributing to it on a policy level. This also means that women are very intricately integrated into militarisation processes in order to then be excluded from high-ranking decision-making processes and agencies linked to it (Kelly 2000: 46). In her work, Enloe amplifies this idea by asking how the military and a militarised society exploit different women to support the system in various functions (2000: 44). According to her, the "patriarchal system" functions best when women in or around the military can even be isolated or divided in their individual supporting role. The "system" automatically disabled solidarity among women against the underlying male power hierarchy. In her example this was done by using notions of women's liberation or empowerment, supposedly granting them equal access to positions and ranks once they entered the military (Enloe 2000: 45). In the same vein, Green points out that while women are vital to the system of militarism, they are by no means equal players. Instead, they can only access roles that are traditionally confined or restricted by similarly spirited norms and regulations as all gendered roles in societies (Green 1999: 87).

Kelly further specifies this by criticising perspectives voiced by some feminists who maintain that women entering the military would be empowered and liberated from otherwise restrictive social norms based on gender constructs. She claims that women's agency within militarised systems is only officially recognised if their activities "resemble traditional male behaviour" in war (Kelly 2000: 46). This understanding not only limits the empowerment women previously saw in joining the military. It also questions the possibility of breaking out of established gender roles by changing to otherwise male-attributed roles to make employing violence legitimate for women as well.

War's different effects on women and men

Considering militarisation happening along gendered lines, the way analysts perceive war affecting people should also follow this substantial differentiation. In the common depiction protagonists of war are mainly men. Women are assigned to passive roles of victims caught in life-threatening situations, or as "pillars of strength", actively keeping families and social life running (Skjelsbaek 1997: 21). Both perceptions convey an essentialist notion of women constantly striving for peace. Between these two extremes, the first perspective is still dominant in the media-induced public expectation and aid discourse. Skjelsbaek complains that it is hard to acquire the necessary data to scrutinise "myths" around "male heroes and female victims" (1997: 21). Yet, such information is vital to understand the mechanisms of essentialising men and women, reducing them to objects within a dominating system. The lack of data serves to disguise women's and men's various agencies, voices, participation or resistance as well as the coping mechanisms they develop during times of armed conflict (Moser and Clark 2001a: 4). Thus, a more simplistic view of male and female roles within conflict persists.

While considering the gender-specific ways of militarisation and their depictions, also influenced by dominant gender-regimes, this should not result in the impression that differences are mere constructions. There are still vital dissimilarities in wars' and conflicts' effects on women and men:

> It is true that men and women share a set of circumstances during armed conflict that exposes them to particularly adverse conditions and to the abuse of their human rights. However, there are certain gender-based risks, dangers and disadvantages, which particularly and disproportionately affect women (Tamayo, cited in Moser and Clark 2001b: 30).

Impressions from various conflicts and regions show that men were more likely to be killed in direct combat, as they constituted the larger part of armies of militias. Though, as wars, especially civil wars shift their strategies and use civilian population for their specific purposes or make attacks on them "an end in itself", more civilian lives are claimed (Skjelsbaek and Smith 2001: 5). As forms of warfare change with new weapons technologies becoming available, the previous division of frontlines and hinterland are being washed away.

Consequently, long-established divisions of male combatants and female civilians who could remain relatively unaffected by war, have to be rethought (Corrin 2004: 210). Other dimensions of war also make clear how important it is to revisit this divide. Acts of sexual violence and torture during war are committed significantly more against women than against men. It is also strategically used and can serve various interests of warring parties (Enloe 2000: 134). In times of HIV/AIDS becoming a major threat, an additional lethal dimension is added onto this kind of violence (Skjelsbaek 1997: 23). Some "types" of violence can only be applied against women, such as forced abortion or impregnation. These are especially relevant and prevalent if wars are fought within a context of identity struggles, where women are used as "markers of identity" and will make them especially vulnerable to sexual violence (Jacobson et al. 2000: 10). Due to lack of or access to different resources and information as well as gender regimes of a militarised society, women and children constitute the majority of internally displaced or refugee population. This fact potentially makes them even more vulnerable to abuse as many are separated from other family members and isolated from supporting networks[1].

While data may exist on how women and men are affected differently by war, details on who is more likely to fall victim of direct combat or rape, most of the every-day life challenges and coping strategies are not accounted for. Therefore, "myths" about gender roles and typical activities of women and men during war are dominating the perception of "gendered battle-fields", elevating and integrating every-day presumptions about gender into the realm of war (Skjelsbaek 1997). Yet, as pointed out above, if war and conflict are integral parts of societies, whatever may happen in war should also follow the established principles of that militarised notion of society. The disparities of women's and men's experiences in war arise from these principles and therefore reveal how basic ideas of gender influence experi-ences and potential agencies during times of armed conflict. To analyse the topic of women's challenges during war and the effects these might have on their identities, women's various involvements in war shall be closely inves-tigated in the following sections.

2.3 Women's roles during war

> The gender dimensions of the battlefield are overshadowed with myths of 'true' men and women (Skjelsbaek 1997: 22).

As discussed above, women have never been excluded from violence and war, but they tend to be differently affected than men. This is to some extent determined by pre-war ideas of gender roles and the way militarisation is incorporating women. Therefore, transgressing such established social and cultural norms could affect or alter ideas of gender roles and influence the whole society. During armed conflict, people live through many different situations of hardship, deprivation or opportunity and develop various sur-vival strategies, not all of which can be analysed in this chapter. As such, the focus shall lie on the different ways women enter direct combat and the many roles they are assigned or expected to fulfil during this time.

---

1 On refugee or internally displaced women's situations see Deng (1998); Gudmundur and Tomasevski (1995); UNHCR (1995).

Women entering armed conflicts

Participation in combat is certainly the most intense and direct form of militarisation. Often no clear dividing lines can be drawn between this and other forms of participation. During civil war and in so-called irregular combat groups or militias, recruitment processes differ fundamentally from established military procedures. Being recruited or volunteering, abduction or gang pressing may, and mostly do overlap. The notion of volunteering is specially contested, as recruitment might be carried out so aggressively, that the target group have little choice but to yield. Lack of alternatives, especially in situation of widespread violence or open warfare coerces girls and young women to join for personal security or material provision as well as supplying families or other dependents with looted goods (Mazurana et al. 2002: 105f.). The devastating economic conditions and widespread destruction of infrastructure as well as extended family ties during the Sierra Leone civil war resulted in many young people, amongst them women, joining one of the fighting factions. Lack of alternatives or war-based loss of the usual patronage support left participation in the war as the only "career prospect" and consequently made the warring factions in the civil war "attractive" to join (Barth 2002). Still, Mazurana et al. claim that for women and girls in countries with civil wars, abduction is the most frequent way of entering into fighting units (2002: 107). As the recruitment mechanisms described by Barth would fit a stereotypically male background better than a female one, in their analysis Mazurana et al. remain within the established notions of gender roles.

With the military or any other fighting group as a "total institution" (Goffman 1961: xiii)[1], women enter an institution that is dominated by a patriarchal mindset. Cordero describes her own entry into *Sendero Luminoso*[2] like this:

1 For further characterisations of "total institutions" also see Barth (2002) and Kaminski (2003).

2 Shining Path, a Maoist Communist organisation in Peru.

> First, we had to assume the identity of 'machos' to increase our competitiveness; second, we had to expand and reproduce our subordinate roles and relations; and third, as if that were not enough, we had to face social and family censure (Cordero 2001: 154).

Whether women take up roles in direct combat or in other "supporting" roles, they are all involved in a male-dominated system, which puts them in certain conditions having to mediate between male-associated combat role and their own female gender roles. These roles do not necessarily change or alter in the framework of an armed group. They are affected by pre-war and "civilian" gender roles. This way, desirable behaviour patterns for women, such as subordination of the self, quiet behaviour in the presence of men and the like are sustained. Some attribute this perpetuation to a lack of opportunities to change during the war. While women have to leave behind certain "traditional attitudes" regarding sexuality and maternity, they have no opportunity to develop norms and values appropriate to their new living conditions (Ibáñez 2001: 121f.). These circumstances hint to the idea that women are indeed taking up roles formerly restricted to men without substantial reflections. Neither does a change on a more general social level regarding gendered constructions of combatants happen, as women still have to adhere to demands related to them from pre-war times.

The struggle to mediate between gendered identities during armed conflict can also be manifested in another way, when women start to take up otherwise male-attributed behaviours outside combat. Within some revolutionary movements, switching of gender roles appeared more manageable than a substantial challenge of gendered attributions. Women claim for themselves to have adopted male roles in wars: "We wanted to be identified as fighters, as men" (Musengezi, cited in Meintjes 2001: 67). Some women employ conventional reference systems of gender stereotypes to be identified as combatants so that they themselves would be identified as not "traditionally" feminine but equipped with male attributes. For the Tigray People's Liberation Front in Ethiopia, Krug describes that women combatants started wearing trousers, smoking in public as well as raising their voices in public or cutting short their hair (2000: 135). They even expressed pride when people did not identify them as women but as part of the (male) combat unit they were travelling with (p. 83). This could serve as protection during combat as well as provide coping strategies for dealing with the new and unknown, sometimes even unintelligible realities of war. Such attempts often even resulted in pressure to prove themselves to male comrades or especially to the other women in the group, living up to stereotyped male ideals of toughness in order to be respected as a combatant (Barth 2002).

Accordingly, these women were not breaking out of conventional gendered role ascriptions but employed them as reference systems or protection and coping mechanisms. Along the idea of military being a "total institution", having the powers to influence perceptions and self-perceptions along with identification processes, women used the available reference points.

Thereby the gender attributes were combined in new ways, pointing to potentially attainable agencies in the context of women's participation in war. These notions are yet to be interrelated with tasks and experiences in the combat group, which has a large influence on the way women identify and relate to combat experiences after war.

Women's possible empowerment beyond combat

Although gender does not necessarily determine all responsibilities or roles in a fighting group, in a lot of instances service tasks and provision of camp and war infrastructure are assigned along otherwise established gendered lines. Such allocations reveal that for women to participate in a fighting group, this does not automatically mean taking up new gender roles. Instead, camp or base maintenance, food collection and preparation, nursing, communications and transport are often assigned to women along the lines of pre-war job segregation. Intelligence gathering as part of communications is often assigned to women due to specific characteristics originating from gender stereotypes. They are expected to be less suspicious when moving across enemy lines either as traders or displaced persons to collect information on troop movement and combat strength. They might also be ordered to camouflage themselves as commercial sex workers to gather intelligence from enemy combatants (Mazurana and Carlson 2004: 16). The tasks assigned additionally to combat responsibilities are sometimes given exclusively to women and as a consequence may exclude them from fighting on the frontline.

In this respect reports from Sierra Leone give a mixed picture, yet mostly emphasising the arms or combat training with later overlapping duties (Mazurana and Carlson 2004: 12)[1]. While task assignments might have differed between factions and, as some interviewees mentioned with reference to the RUF/SL, even between combat units, the above depictions give the impression that infrastructure or service assignments additionally to combat were more likely to happen with women. As such, roles of women as combatants and "camp followers" overlapped, while men would mostly be attributed to fewer "domestic" service roles (Mazurana et al. 2002: 111). The way women interpret these multiple functions and activities during war shapes their identity as well. This is one point of gendered discourse of social changes during war as men tended to have less overlapping combat and service demands and roles. At the same time, the topic of overlapping duties and assignments is vital especially for women's post-war perspective on their participation in conflict and the atrocities linked to it[2].

Considering the above, potentials of changes of gender roles through participation in combat appear to be limited. The overall male-dominated military system incorporates women and men into a "total institution", limiting negotiation space of new identities (Enloe 2000: 207). The available reference systems are the conventional gender ideas and stereotypes. Within such institutions, substantial changes of ascribed roles and potential identifications are disabled, so that no new gendered identities can be developed. In this notion, looking at the distribution of tasks in a combat group containing women, they find themselves constrained in the established roles of service providers. This sphere of their participation in war is prominent and may contribute to the perception that little or no substantial changes of gendered roles take place even by women's direct participation in armed conflict.

Women's participation in war can take many forms, some of which have been described above. However this involvement is characterised, mere participation does not necessarily result in empowerment through the challenging established gender roles (D'Amico 1998: 120). Some armed groups, especially communist-inspired revolutionary movements emphasise women's empowerment and gender equality and even educate their members on these topics as part of their ideological indoctrination[3]. According to Barth, even

---

1 See chapter 1.3.

2 For the post-war consequences of overlapping chores in Sierra Leone see chapters 1.3 and 4.2.

3 Documented, for example for the conflicts in Ethiopia in Krug (2000); Kashmir, Sri Lanka, Nepal and Haiti in Meintjes et al. (2001); or for Eritrea in Zimprich (1996).

this education and propaganda within and outside the movement might support long-term changes of gender roles. While it may strengthen women's status during the fighting, such ideology does not necessarily secure peacetime changes in the society or within the legal framework (Barth 2002).

Given the intricate connection of established overarching gender roles with the militarised spheres of armed combat, it appears questionable whether shifts or changes of gender roles could occur during fighting. Rather, established roles are taken and are newly combined by and within the roles of women participating in combat and in service roles. These new combinations, employed as protection or coping mechanisms, could foster a shift or challenge, but no substantial change. Meintjes et al. even make a conscious effort for women's empowerment during the conflict a prerequisite to substantial changes of women's rights after the war: "The real opportunity for planting seeds for transformation is during wartime, in conditions of conflict" (2001: 10). In a similar understanding, Bop points out that there are actual organisational structures necessary to establish and secure the potential long-term challenges for women's empowerment in and after armed conflict. Otherwise, even if willing, women would not be able to even secure the new roles they attained during the war (Bop 2001: 33).

The persistence of ideas of femininity and gendered division of tasks rather hint to Enloe's claim that women were only allowed within the militarised system, when they served the system's interest or complimented the "dominant masculine culture" (2000: 212).

2.4 Women after the conflict

Considering the above discussion on the intricate relationships between conflict and society, including the transcending gender roles, it is questionable to what extent processes of change can be induced by wars. While women combatants adhere to some established gender roles, during armed struggle they also mediate them with otherwise male-dominated ones which they are sometimes even striving to attain. In comparing different conflict settings, Pankhurst points to the fact that such processes are highly influenced by the "socialising" conditions participants experience during the conflict (2004: 31). Different variables may influence the outcome and the potential perpetuation of war's influences on social dynamics and gender relations. Cockburn argues that war has multi-facetted impacts on men and women, cumulating differently with individual actors. As such, potential changes in one sphere of life might be met by re-strengthening traditions in another, leading to tensions about the further development of social and cultural issues. Consequently, no generalisation can be made on how wars are affecting identities or gender relations (Cockburn 2001: 26).

In the following, women combatants' experiences after the conflict shall be analysed, heeding the above cautions. Being exposed to combat and having to mediate or negotiate the newly assigned roles, women could be facing subsequent challenges with integration into civilian life. They may face pressure to fulfil social expectations, some of which may (re-) establish traditional ideas. Broadening the perspective from established gender roles, women in specific circumstances also took up roles and performed tasks that breached these roles. Consequently, while social processes are working to support healing and integration processes, some war-time influences may be disabling the return to traditional roles and ideas and instead open up other perspectives.

With observations from different conflict settings the background question shall be whether (assumed) wartime or post-conflict changes can be perpetuated or manifested with a political and policy interest in securing women's rights (e.g. Barth 2002; Molyneux 1985). These intentions and analyses may be prone to see participation in war as an empowering experience in itself, yet, whether women can or do actually aim for such empowerment shall be questioned below. In a first step of the analysis, some clearly political voices aiming at the establishment of women's equal rights shall be introduced to prepare the ground for broader analysis of their interpretation of war-time effects on identification and gender roles.

The aftermath of women's involvement in war

Due to war-related destruction of infrastructure and shifts of providing roles, women are much more under pressure to perform and secure the livelihood of their families or dependents. Considering these demands, from the outside perspective some women seem to be returning as quickly as possible to pre-war responsibilities. Western feminists are often disappointed by such developments, as they seem to imply that war did not change roles and responsibilities, or only changed them temporarily (Macdonald 1987: 9f.). While the armed conflict lasted women appear to be part of it, seemed to get involved in new tasks and were assigned new roles, which appeared to sometimes call for a longer-term impact on women's behaviour, self-image and self-esteem. This should especially count for women who participated in the fighting as combatants, having been exposed to new experiences, impressions and gained new insights. With the ensuing peace process, many of these "achievements" seem to be forgotten or deliberately pushed back. Krug reports this even for cases in which an armed movement was explicitly supporting women's empowerment and educating their members on these and related topics. Quite the opposite happened after the end of the conflict. Often, even comrades of the war expected women to return to their "traditional" roles and responsibilities (Krug 2000: 79).

Meintjes et al. claim that with regard to women's exposure to different kinds of violence and suppression there is no aftermath for women as "after the conflict is before the conflict" (2001: 3). This perspective implies that within a given society norms and regulations concerning women's and men's roles are so entrenched that war cannot have a substantially changing effect on them. As discussed in 2.2, it should be remembered that post-conflict processes are also guided by societies' ideas of militarisation and post-conflict coping mechanisms. They should provide socially acceptable coping strategies, ways and procedures to deal with experiences of war. These are guided by established and therefore conservative ideas.

From a women's rights' perspective, peace has in some instances been identified as a "disappointment" (Barth 2002), and strategies have been developed on how to secure "the *rights* they won on the battlefield, notably *equality* with men" (Bop 2001: 31, emphases added). Together with other authors[1], Bop obviously does not only take up a rights-based approach towards the situation of women, but also assumes that a war will substantially empower women.

In the following section, questions shall be posed as to whether the (pro-)claimed empowering experiences of a war can actually lead to changes of gender roles and whether these could be sustained in a post-conflict environment. For this purpose, different conflict settings shall serve as reference

1 See especially Afshar and Eade (2004); Lorentzen and Turpin (1998); Meintjes et al. (2001); Moser and Clark (2001a).

to possible experiences, all highlighting specific aspects of the transition from war to peace.

Changing or re-establishing pre-war gender roles

Reflecting on the above discussion, it seems questionable whether gender roles do substantially change during war, even for those women directly involved in combat.

Women combatants find themselves in changing circumstances once the war is over. In Latin America women have fought in all of the numerous wars on the continent, with some of the movements they participated in having explicit ideologies supporting the empowerment of women. After the war, many of these women could not implement changes in their lives in the way they had been promised. On the contrary, they suffered from results of the long-term violence that had established increasing misogyny and atrocities against women due to the specific targeting of women as the "community signifiers" by different militias (Leslie 2001). Social stress and disappointments from the war spread aggressive behaviour and made violence more acceptable. Taken together, the increase of (public and private) violence against women as well as its acceptability should not be surprising (Turpin 1998: 7).

Similarly, female combatants in Russia who had fought in World War II were "redefined and re-feminised" as mothers (Enloe 2000: 217). While generally their contributions to the war's victory were acknowledged in public, different expectations were raised towards individual women. In Vietnam, female ex-combatants were also praised collectively. However, individually they were expected to rebuild the country by bearing children. Those who remained childless as a result of the war became "an embarrassment" to the nation (Enloe 2000: 225). Under a different topic, Meintjes et al. point to the economic threats women's empowerment might mean to older generations who particularly rely on young women's labour for resources and therefore try to re-establish "traditions" serving this end[1] (2001: 13).

A different war-time activity, not directly related to participation in the fighting, but with survival mechanisms around it, is 'attack trade'. Due to

1 In Sierra Leone, *Sande* plays a considerable role in this economic notion of *gerontocracy* (Fuest 1999; Richards et al. 2004).

women moving around more freely during war, men often being the main targets of attack, or simply by necessity of providing for their family, trade often constitutes or becomes a female occupation during war, if it was not already before the war (*Fatu*).

Crossing enemy lines or providing combatants with goods involves taking extra risks, but this may also secure the own and the family's survival, besides often being the only and lucrative source of income (Zdunnek 2002: 146f.). While women take up additional responsibilities, work and risks, at the same time attack trade might offer new experiences, insights and chances for women to move around more than previously, developing new networks or expanding long established ones. New initiatives can result from such enterprises, like savings or small-scale credit schemes. Examples from Chad and Colombia show how these activities can result in more social and economic participation of women in public and generated a feeling of empowerment among the women involved (Cockburn 2001: 26f.). Developments like these can also be observed with refugees and internally displaced women in Sierra Leone. In camps they were exposed to new social contexts, after loosing a lot of personal ties due to war and displacement. With international interventions and educational programmes as well as general exposure to other living conditions and information, some women became aware of and used changed power relations. After the war ended, some were reluctant to leave behind the newly established networks, which had supported the feeling of change and sometimes even empowerment (Meintjes et al. 2001: 16).

While securing opportunities for survival and family support, women ran the risk of upsetting norms and as a consequence may be accused of immoral behaviour or even prostitution, especially in the case of trade women who are travelling long distances (Zdunnek 2002: 159). Notwithstanding, these cases are apparent and widespread. "Sex for survival" is indeed an option to which a lot of young women feel compelled due to lack of income generating alternatives. Strategic relationships to resourceful men can ensure the survival of oneself and dependents but at the same time can lead to abusive relationships due to the power relations involved. In these cases women clearly breach ideas of norms and moral. Over all, Zdunnek claims, women's achievements and sacrifices for their family or dependents are rarely generally acknowledged or appreciated but are instead "trivialised" (1997: 32).

The transformation process towards peace also holds specifically gendered possibilities for combatants. For example, cleansing ceremonies to ease the ritual (re-) entry into civilian life, washing away guilt or the blood of enemies, have been reported in many African societies. They also take place in the context of *Poro* in Sierra Leone (*Momoh*; Richards et al. 2003). These rituals are part of socially and spiritually established coping mechanisms in times of war. They do not only serve the individual who is cleansed, but are part of communal coping strategies, inadvertently (re-) establishing "traditional" power relationships (Bennett et al. 1995: 18). As in the case of Sierra Leone, these ceremonies have usually been restricted to men (Bop 2001: 29). Women find it much harder to attain such cleansing and therefore do not enjoy the benefit of eased reintegration (Alden 2002: 352). While specific cleansing rituals seem unattainable for young women and girls who had not been initiated into female sodalities before or during the war were in some places encouraged to go through the process in order to support their reacceptance into a local community. However McKay and Mazurana assert that these processes would "reinforce patriarchy and oppressive gender roles" as well as "violate the human rights of women and girls" (2004: 50).

Cases like these reveal the influence of pre-war gendered ideas on people who are accepted perpetrators of violence. While male combatants can benefit from ritual ceremonies easing their entry into civilian life, women combatants do not have these options. If they are nevertheless trying to reintegrate, as in the case of initiation into female sodalities, they have to succumb to the "patriarchal" notions of gender roles. Thereby they inadvertently condemn their own wartime breaches of established gender roles. Some might embrace such options and stand for the upkeep of "traditional" views and practices, while others may decide not to do so (Meintjes 2001: 68).

The processes described above show the varying reintegration possibilities that function along gendered lines. While some women feel they have been positively affected by their experience in the military or during fighting, they may decide not to reinforce the implied changes as they meet a society that does not necessarily acknowledge or approve of these influences. The wider society has obviously also been influenced by war, but not necessarily in the same way. These considerations make the establishment of substantially changed gender roles after the war quite unlikely (Bop 2001: 20). El-Bushra attributes this to the fact that women did take up responsibilities and new roles, so on a personal level changes in self-images occurred; yet women were not granted the corresponding power within the wider society, reflected in legal change or access to political representation. This way, differences between individual self-perception and socially assigned roles and behaviour could occur, which then prohibited substantial changes of gender roles (El-Bushra 2004: 163).

These notions convey the challenge some female combatants might face after the fighting is over. They might have cast off established sets of values or norms by joining a fighting force, yet they have no guarantee that a post-conflict situation will acknowledge or accommodate these changes (Gedalof 1999: 181). Quite the contrary, some of the former combatants might find themselves in less advantageous positions after the war than before the war. A peace process means transformation in a war-affected society. This might lead to a feeling of insecurity or instability in which demands of empowerment or equality of women could be interpreted as a threat, for basic power divisions in society would simultaneously be questioned. This is why tendencies of "re-traditionalisation" of women's roles and responsibilities could serve as a measure against growing insecurity (Badran 1995: 22f.). As discussed in 2.1, it has been pointed out by many authors that women will find it harder to change or contest these "traditional" notions of identities if they or their bodies serve as symbols of the community (Yuval-Davis 1992: 8f.).

Within this wider discourse of post-conflict societies male-attributed gender roles also face challenges. In many societies men are believed to be the main economic providers for and decision makers within the family. Due to destruction caused by war, men can often not fulfil these ideals and experience stress, loss of control and respect. In these situations, some men become violent or depressed, inhibiting them even more with regard to adjusting to the new post-conflict situation (Ibáñez 2001: 128). This situation can even be exacerbated if men were involved as combatants and as such lost the war or were left disabled in any way. As a consequence, manhood and masculinity could be questioned or regarded as weakened (Sideris 2001: 51f.). All these changes could happen after men's stereotypical gender roles had been reaffirmed during the war due to militarisation taking place along the corresponding gendered lines. In this notion, Barth points out that the challenges men face after war regarding psychological issues, identities and gender roles are not yet adequately investigated (2002)[1].

The observations above reveal the difficult situations women combatants find themselves in after the war. They have new and different hopes and expectations but meet a society that is tentatively trying to re-establish norms and regulations to stabilise itself. In such difficult conditions, analysts still claim that in some cases women can "capitalise" on a weak or instable state by strongly pushing for their own interests (Kandiyoti 1991: 140). This may particularly be the case in the immediate aftermath of the war, as a society is regarded by some to be more fluid and flexible at this time. Essentially society could accommodate changes after a war, when some norms and values are subject to (social and cultural) re-negotiations (Eade 2004).

While so far communities and societies have been analysed as isolated from an international discourse, the next section shall introduce this dimension, as it is strongly interlinked with the notion of "capitalising" on supposedly more fluid social discourses in a post-conflict setting. In Sierra Leone, this concept is referred to as the "window of opportunity" after the end of the civil war and is substantially supported by international women's right's discourses.

Against a backlash: Maintaining empowerment

In whatever way, certainly the experience of combat and violence did affect the participating women and men. Also, changing conditions lead people to perform different tasks to cope with war's destructive effects. As such, it can be assumed that changes in self-images, if not even social roles, did occur, affecting individual concepts of identification and those of whole groups. Yet, developments happening during war appear to be hard to sustain, especially in the context of women's empowerment. Meintjes contemplates whether this results from the fact that women might not be struggling hard enough or not in an organised way that could help secure the assumed changes (2001: 76). Nevertheless, in a post-conflict situation a lot of women find themselves occupied with the struggle to secure their livelihood, for example reflected in the rise of female-headed households during and after a war.

---

1 See also chapter 3.2 on men and masculinities after war.

Women's economic empowerment is often seen as good entry point to change the social position of women in a community. Supported by the academic discourse, this topic features high on the agendas of organisations involved in post-conflict situations. They try to engage women in economic activities, income generation projects, vocational training or micro-credit schemes of various kinds. These are not always accompanied by a broader information or "educational" project, and this is the point El-Bushra sees as crucial for the projects' quickly fading effects on women's self-perception as well as their standing in society. Social and cultural "sensitisation" are perceived to enable sustainable changes in this area (El-Bushra 2004: 165). Leslie even explicitly distinguishes between personal and social as well as political spheres of women's empowerment. In her perspective, the introduction of the political sphere necessitates the inclusion of all other groups in society, to bear witness and support potential changes (Leslie 2001: 56). Moser and Clark, focusing on women ex-combatants, also reflect on this more socially oriented approach. Considering their potential stigmatisation resulting from the war, women ex-combatants should discuss their experiences and try to re-interpret them in positive ways. In this process, changes and challenges from and within the wider community should be integrated. Only this way, according to the authors, could these women "maintain their independence and leadership" (Moser and Clark 2001b: 34).

Undoubtedly, such processes are quite hard to analyse and therefore to implement, as war experiences are always very diverse and culturally specific. Gender relations are affected in multiple ways by different wars. The way women could "capitalise" on a post-conflict situation also differs substantially depending on the roles and responsibilities taken up during war and their situation before and after the war. Regarding the diversity of conditions and influences, no real predictions can be made about how gender relations will develop after an armed conflict ends. Nonetheless, many possibilities and options should be open and available, once they were considered and supported from the outside (Skjelsbaek 2001).

Such support greatly draws on the ideas introduced above. While not all organisations involved in post-conflict settings may depict these notions clearly, Bouta et al. give clear directions in the case of the World Bank:

> At the minimum, the Bank could support women and men to sustain the roles, positions, skills, and opportunities gained during conflict in the post-conflict phase […] For gender-related interventions in conflict-affected countries *timing* is crucial. […] the transition phase from war to peace offers the best moment to sustain gender role changes and to lay the basis for future gender relations. It is here, when women and men have not yet returned to stability, that gender relations are still in the process of being redefined (Bouta et al. 2005: 142, emphasis in original).

Assuming questionable wartime changes of gender roles, "interventions" are proposed, using a proclaimed "window of opportunity" in the transition from war to peace. The potential benefits of such an intervention in this area are based on security issues as well as social development ideas. As Mackay puts it:

> A 'peace' that neglects the interest of a large part of the community or that supports, reconstructs or in some cases strengthens the inequalities in the power structure […] can not truly be called a peace worth having – and is unlikely to be sustainable (2004: 107).

Consequently, in the interest of "sustainable peace" women's integration into the peace process and post-conflict reconstruction is regarded as essential. Development planners and practitioners are therefore trying to support women in roles, which they attained during war, even if in the context of so-called coping strategies. Assuming women were equal during fighting, after the war they "just lost the rights" they had previously gained during combat (Bop 2001: 31). Projects therefore aim to increase women's visibility and participation in public or in economic concerns. With regard to the above discussion, such projects may aim at uncertain, constructed or construed developments of women's self-perception and post-war gender relations, rather than what is genuine or actually attainable.

2.5 Summary

> What happens if our identities 'fail', and might such failures provide opportunities for subversive *re*constructions of identity? Perhaps those reconstructions, as subversive as they may seem, will end up cohering into identity formations, which are just as oppressive in their own way. How can we tell what is subversion and what merely consolidates power? And what degree of choice do we have about how we 'do' our identities? (Salih 2002: 2f., emphasis in original)

Salih summarises the problematic situation women find themselves in after armed conflict, especially women ex-combatants striving for change. Chances are there to change; but at the same time the available reference systems of people are still dominated by established thoughts and ideas. Considering that militarisation and ideologies surrounding conflicts and wars are part of most societies, how can these wars lead to substantial changes in self-perceptions or gender roles? Even if women (can) access new tasks, responsibilities and maybe empowering experiences and new opportunities leading to shifts of individual (gender) identities, this does not mean substantial re-discussion of gender roles as part of concepts of individual and group identities (Sideris 2001: 52).

El-Bushra discusses these developments specifically for women ex-combatants who she claims are under higher pressure to perform according to pre-war realities or ideals. This again is part of the pre-conflict gendered power conditions (El-Bushra 2004: 164).

Considering the diversity of wars, societies and experiences of women and men, different potentials and gains as well as losses would be possible, also considering challenges or discussions of (lived) gender roles (Bop 2001: 23). Yet, the remaining question is whether these women and men indeed aim at such changes or would actually prefer returning to pre-war conditions, which they might have never substantially questioned as a whole system, but only parts of it. In a related study, Skjelsbaek highlights three different ways in which femininity and women's self-images were influenced by war (2001). Following the conflict, women in various settings perceived their femininity either as victimised, liberated or remaining "conservative", as in not substantially changed. According to the authors this depended on the ideological foundations of the mobilisation and the ensuing policies and practices towards women, or on “how the conflict was organised along gendered lines” (Skjelsbaek and Smith 2001: 9).

With war affecting women very differently, the introduction of “gender-related interventions” cited above (Bouta et al. 2005: 142), outside influences hope to take a shaping influence on the perception and desirability of evolving gender relations. While it remains to be seen whether the potential developments indicated in this chapter can be transferred into the Sierra Leonean context, outside influences are certainly taking their chance to influencing gender relations. One of the major organisations doing so shall be introduced in the next chapter.

3 Women and the Demobilisation process of Sierra Leone

In the previous chapter, the focus lay on theoretical considerations of the impact war has on women, their self-image and on gender relations. In this chapter, light shall be shed on the way international organisations interact with this topic directly after the war, exemplified in the Disarmament, Demobilisation and Reintegration programme of Sierra Leone. In preparation, the first part of this chapter shall introduce gender mainstreaming as a systematic tool aiming at gender equality. The processes and discourses around this concept are analysed within the UN system with a specific focus on agencies dealing with peacekeeping and disarmament. In this light, the second part shall discuss the concept of DDR in its specific setting of Sierra Leone, with short references to other UN programmes. The institutional set-up of the UN system in Sierra Leone shall be introduced in the context of this Demobilisation example. In a third step, the categories of eligibility for accessing the programme will be reflected upon, analysing potential messages on gender roles in order to prepare for the analysis of women's reactions to them in the following chapter.

3.1 Women and gender mainstreaming in the UN

While many different institutions such as national governments or local organisations are involved in post-conflict work, the main emphasis in this chapter, regarding organisations and institutions, lies on the United Nations. Agencies and organisations within the UN system are specialised on (policy-relevant) research and on implementation of peacekeeping and peace building measures, of which DDR is a part (Colletta et al. 1996). At the same time, money for such projects is primarily made available within the wider UN sphere and therefore it can be regarded as one of the major donors in the area of post-conflict work. The funds are either generated within the system or channelled through it towards partner or implementing organisations.

Many controversial views exist on these recipient organisations that are labelled NGOs, Community Based Organisations (CBOs) or grassroots organisations. These are interwoven regarding political influence, accountability and funding procedures. As conflict transformation and peacekeeping increased as well as humanitarian aid shifted in the wake of the cold war, potential roles for civil society became more obvious and approachable. Reacting to these changes, many relief and aid agencies have been broadening their attention to include cooperation around UN peacekeeping operations. Consequently, some authors speak of the "internationalisation" of disaster or conflict work (Reimann 2000: 13) and of the "internationalisation" of conflicts themselves and of their supporting mechanisms (Nordstrom 2001).

The variety and multitude of NGOs that can be observed, especially when adding local and grassroots organisations to the number of INGOs working in a country, points to the necessity of coordination and regulation. As Boutros-Ghali already pointed out in "An Agenda for Peace" with reference to DDR programmes: "if UN efforts are to succeed, the roles of the various players need to be carefully coordinated" (1992: paragraph 81). In the apparent diversity, this coordination would obviously be difficult to achieve, especially when looking at the global scale of such a challenge; but donor agencies do take an active interest, which can be reflected in multiple ways. For example, the UN Office for the Coordination of Humanitarian Affairs (OCHA) was created to support such coordination of relief efforts on the ground in emergency situations; however, it has limited scopes to do so. This includes internal politics as other UN agencies saw their autonomy threatened by a separate agency having influence on them. As the result of this "turf war", OCHA's funding and authority were cut down to become merely marginal (Byman 2001: 102). In a similar notion, the powers connected to financing projects and the implementing organisations' partial or total dependency on funding, thematic emphases can be included into or excluded from the funding cycles, depending on the donor's preferences and political considerations. Meintjes even refers to such interrelations as donors "dictating an NGO's agenda" (2001: 74), with the effect of reducing aid organisations to "contractors" (Richmond 2003: 3). Smaller national or local but even international NGOs therefore tend to follow the large donor organisations' lead in their definitions of priorities, concepts and vocabulary (Richter-Lyonette 2004: 263f.).

With these interdependencies of structures, ideas and finances, focussing on the UN sphere shall serve as a reference to gain an impression of the current discourse on gender issues in the international community. In the present circumstances, concentrating on a multi-facetted concept like gender mainstreaming, an all-encompassing critique of its integration into the UN would surpass the scope of this book. Therefore, in the following discussion, the focus shall lie on selected areas such as the conceptual framing of gender mainstreaming and the integration and promotion of female personnel. This is referred to as gender balance, regarded by many analysts in- and outside of the UN system as an important indicator for internal gender policies and an organisation's mainstreaming determination (Mazurana et al. 2005b: 13f.)[1].

The gender mainstreaming concepts in the UN system

Gender mainstreaming has become a central issue in public discourses; especially international bodies and the aid industry[2] have been working with this concept for more than a decade. Since the "United Nations Fourth World Conference on Women" in Beijing in 1995, all UN organisations are required to employ gender mainstreaming as a strategy to reach gender equity and equality. As such, it features as a central part of the "Beijing Platform for Action". The whole concept can be narrowed down to two points:

1. The analysis of issues and the formulation of policy options are informed by consideration of gender differences and inequalities;
2. opportunities are sought to narrow gender gaps and support greater equality between women and men" (OSAGI 2002: 1f.).

Gender analysis is identified as the starting point in the Beijing Platform for Action, and it is here, where most analysts see shortcomings in the implementation of the guidelines and procedures put forward by some of the highest policy making institutions of the UN. Officially, all UN organisations,

1 See also Raven-Roberts 2005.

2 The term "aid industry" or "humanitarian industry" refers to processes of "neo-liberalisation", putting formerly humanitarian or aid work under the pressure of (political) economic rationale (Le Sage 1998: 29).

institutions and departments are required to develop and implement a gender action plan, which is supposed to mainstream gender into its own structures and into the policies and programmes. The requirements also include that cooperation or implementation partners (IP's) are obliged to follow gender mainstreaming policies. This implies the establishment of gender as a cross-cutting issue, a status that has been re-affirmed by resolutions, conventions and policy documents. As a consequence, gender mainstreaming, as a concept, policy and strategy should be included in all activities and in any organisation within the UN system. This approach is quite the opposite of previous UN strategies concerning women, having previously been sidelined into special departments or councils, separate from the every-day work in the organisations (Olsson 1999: 2).

Despite of the use of the term "gender", often interpretations limit its scope to the inclusion of women, substituting or equating it to affirmative action for women. Obviously, gender analyses can highlight how women are put at the disadvantage, but this notion sidelines the employment of gender as an analytical tool and therefore also leads to the omission of male perspectives as well as to the incorporation of the goal behind the mainstreaming: supporting greater equality between women and men.

As such, gender mainstreaming does not oppose the support of women's organisations or interests, but can be an integral part of bridging the gender gaps (OSAGI 2002: 2). This superficially observed contradiction poses some difficulty for the institutions and staff working with gender. In line with the first perspective, some staff claim that with gender mainstreaming being employed all women-focussed projects should end, while the UN Office of the Special Advisor to the Secretary-General on Gender Issues and Advancement of Women (OSAGI) points out that one is no substitute for the other, both practices having their relevance (2002). As Mazurana et al. stress, that the two concepts should be viewed as complementary, as one cannot work successfully without the other (2005b: 13, 15).

Within the area of peace operations, the inclusion of new concepts, such as gender mainstreaming, are determined by long-standing structures and established procedures of the UN as well as international relations. Peace building, understood as more than military observation of a bilateral peace agreement, was long based on "An Agenda for Peace" by Boutros-Ghali (1992). According to Väyrynen, peacekeeping operations are ideologically based on this notion, incorporating aspects of "Modernity", of clear-cut boundaries between war and peace and other dichotomies, thereby implying the same binary oppositions for combatant and civilian, women and men (Väyrynen 2004: 135). At the same time, a "rational problem-solving attitude" is laid down as the basic concept for UN organisations and staff to analyse and work on wars and peace building or keeping (p. 127f.). From the author's point of view, UN peace operations combine "professional and expert knowledge" on war, arms and policies with "managerial functions" to administer a population defined by the state territory through building rationally functioning state institutions[1] (p. 131). As a consequence, the UN system appears to be caught in dichotomies concerning its policies and structures.

Within UN peacekeeping and related areas, women or gender topics were not systematically included until the 1990's. The "Windhoek Declaration" and the "Namibia Plan of Action" (UNTAG 2000) are explicit documents with this end, along with the Security Council Resolution 1325 on "Women, Peace and Security" in 2000, that put the integration of women into peace building on the agenda. Both documents draw on the rights-based approach and point out how the inclusion of women can benefit peace building and peace-keeping. While Resolution 1325 names targets and concepts, the Namibia Plan of Action goes into procedural details and points to shortcomings of the past, the need to clarify capacities, competence and reporting requirements due to an observed lack of communication in the horizontal as well as vertical structures of UN organisations (UNTAG 2000, Paragraph 7).

While these documents have been received positively by some, others criticise the "functionalising" and "rationalising" of women for the cause of peace. As such, these documents maintain the previous "add women and stir" attitude (Wharton 2005: 4) often found in organisations facing the call for gender mainstreaming. With UN agencies' conceptual background in modernity, gender discourses in the relevant institutions are still marked by notions of responding to the specific vulnerability of women. Following this

1 Placing the state at the centre of activities and as the main counterpart for UN's work, along ideas of Modernity, may sometimes leave the UN without the appropriately accountable partner, especially in cases of "shadow states" like Sierra Leone (Reno 2001). This approach, according to Nordstrom, seems inappropriate in times of internationalised conflicts and conflict's beneficiaries, where nation states are not the only actors (Nordstrom 2001).

interpretation, the author points out, even the much-cited Security Council Resolution 1325 and the Windhoek Declaration draw on such lines:

> Women have been denied access and participation in peace building [...] Women have been denied their full role in [...] peace support operations both nationally and internationally, and the gender dimension in peace processes has not been adequately addressed (Wharton 2005: 137).

Additionally, as Vincent points out, notions of "liberal individualism" which in her understanding of gender should accompany the mainstreaming process, do not at all succeed to enter the policy or implementation sphere (2003: 6).

While acknowledging the importance and potential benefit of including women in peace building and peacekeeping operations, in the understanding of the UN, gender is still limited to binary oppositions of men and women, with gender mainstreaming equalling the inclusion of women. Women's rights are recognised as equal, nonetheless they are still perceived to need support and protection, lacking their own voices and agencies. With such an understanding, a substantial challenge of epistemology and essentialising ideologies of women and men within the UN system are perceived as unnecessary. Therefore, from a system-inherent perspective, structures and power relations within the UN appear to not need questioning (Väyrynen 2004: 138f.).

On a similar note, problems of accountability and evaluation of gender-related issues have not yet been consistently resolved. While reports are required to be written and performance on gender mainstreaming issues is included in the UN "Performance Appraisal System" of every staff member (Marcaillou 2003: 51), the real impact on every-day work is still questionable. Additionally, despite the regular monitoring and evaluation practices, there are no established criteria for measurements of progress or success of "engendered projects" yet (Puechguirbal 2003: 127). This might not only be linked to conceptual problems, but also to the fact that due to financing procedures "quick impact projects" are preferred by many organisations, whereas projects with the explicit incorporation of gender take longer time. According to Richter-Lyonette, these should affect behavioural patterns and "local traditions", making interventions harder and impacts more difficult to measure (2004: 271).

As a consequence, Puechguirbal asserts that changes required by gender mainstreaming could only be achieved with the persistent support of an individual senior bureaucrat in an organisation or mission[1], otherwise "all gender-related initiatives are doomed to fail in the long run" (2003b: 127).

Some justifications for not pushing too much for gender mainstreaming are brought forward, pointing to the "intimate cultural affairs" that could be affected by consistent gender programming, touching on some aspects at the very core of collective or community values (Peterson, cited in Olsson 1999: 31). Meintjes points out that these are serious considerations as some national governments, counterparts of the UN, could fear upsetting established power relationships, potentially leading to social insecurity and destabilisation (Meintjes 2001: 69). Yet, in an argument such as the above social impacts or indirect effects of other, "un-gendered" or "gender-neutral" programmes are not seen as critical at all (Ollson 2005: 168). Nevertheless, having pointed out the inter-governmental characteristics of the UN, these concerns need to be taken into account by the locally based personnel.

Gender mainstreaming in peace building agencies

The broad terms of peacekeeping and peace building serve as overarching concepts of UN missions and programmes in countries, for which the organisation has been mandated by the Security Council (and in coordination with local governments) to observe or even secure a peace agreement between (former) warring parties. Support for war-to-peace transition is the focus besides the military component. One of the main tasks, especially in cases of long-term or civil conflict, is demilitarisation and demobilisation of militarised societies (Mazurana 2004: 67)[2]. This is encompassed by the DDR programmes, usually lead by a UN mission and embedded into a broader framework of long-term peace and arms control policy, advised on by research bodies in- and outside of the UN[3].

The major organisations involved in this area are DPKO and the respective UN country missions, established ad-hoc by UN Security Council reso-

1 Characteristically for an administration of civil service, UN institutions are stratified by a strict hierarchy, in which influence can hardly be exerted bottom-up, but only top-down (*Anna*; Abdela 2004: 93).

2 See also Colletta et al. (1996); Kingma (2000); Knight and Özerdem (2004).

3 Such as the United Nations Institute for Disarmament Research (UNIDIR) in Geneva, Switzerland, or the Pearson Peacekeeping Centre (PPC) in Cornwallis, Canada.

lutions. Their staff is, to certain extent, experienced from previous missions[1] or come from other organisations working in related areas. With this ad-hoc establishment of missions and national, regional and international political interests inherently becoming part of them, problems are to be expected[2]. A UN peacekeeper in Kosovo points to some of these problems:

> [n]o clear sense of purpose; muddled and contradictory goals and objectives crafted by amateurs, implemented by incompetents; and defended by bureaucrats whose sole purpose in life is to move up the food chain (cited in Abdela 2004: 94).

Peacekeeping operations, located in the supposedly "exclusively" male policy domain of international relations (Tickner 1999), have over time developed beyond simply sending soldiers to observe bilateral peace agreements. Civilian components of the mission have become more important over time. With the advent of so-called "wider-", "multi-dimensional" or "second-generation" peacekeeping in the early 1990's, the tasks of UN mission were broadened to include humanitarian aid as well as demobilisation elements. These were emphasised even more when the conceptual shift occurred to what was later to be termed "third-generation" peacekeeping, when even more non-military actors were involved as the civilian, humanitarian and political stabilisation components became more prominent since the mid 1990's (Debiel 2002: 475–9; Katayanagi 2002: 42–53).

Following these trends, the inclusion of "male and female perspectives" in a country's and society's development appears conclusive (Olsson 1999: 3f.). Compared to the overall UN system, the number of women working in these organisations is quite very small. While gender balance might have been achieved in the UN headquarters of the respective organisations, on the ground the situation remains biased towards a substantially higher proportion of men (Mazurana et al. 2005: 14). On the first look this seems surprising, as in many UN missions the civilian (and traditionally more female-represented) component is quite substantial (Olsson 1999: 9f.). Yet, the overall organisational culture of the UN is identified by many researchers as

---

1 As Abdela points out, senior posts in peace missions are subject to "diplomatic trade", with many high-ranking personnel moving from one mission to the next (2004: 93f.).

2 For a case study on Sierra Leone, see Malan et al. (2002); on Somalia see, amongst others, Debiel (2002: 282ff.).

male-dominated[1], with the personal ties of established (male) personnel leading to recruitment and promotion procedures resembling "old boys' networks" (Olsson 1999: 12).

While criticising the UN, it is important to note that these conditions are only reflecting those of its member states. Most of them show both horizontal and vertical segregation of jobs along gendered lines. The field of policy developments, military or security issues can be termed nearly exclusively male[2]. In the actual, on the ground peacekeeping work of soldiers, Military Observers (MilObs) and Civil Police (CivPol), women are represented in even smaller numbers. When the UN calls upon its members to provide peacekeepers, it may specifically call for the participation of women. Often, the countries do not follow this call or may not even be able to do so as they do not have women in respective positions in their national military or police force (Beilstein 1998: 143).

Some voices are defending such gender-segregated working conditions due to local requirements in which "women in leadership posts would be 'alien to local culture and tradition'" (Abdela 2004: 91). However Stiehm points out that most of these statements are found to be assumptions made by male "UN bureaucrats" rather than requests voiced by a mission's "host society" (1997: 43).

Despite the above criticism of neglecting gender mainstreaming in internal structures and the absence of women within the organisations, some UN organisations are working on integrating this concept into their structures and programming procedures. Like other UN institutions, DPKO also had to develop gender-training tools using a rights-based approach as part of its gender mainstreaming efforts. As in the case of Sierra Leone, the "gender unit" was included in the post-arrival training of peacekeepers in various countries and UN missions. Yet, despite these efforts, Puechguirbal reports that most peacekeepers "do not recollect gender training, but they do remember logistics training, how to use a radio in the field, what to do in case of hostage taking and the amount of monthly subsistence allowance they receive" (2003b: 123). This is not only reflecting the meaning peacekeepers

1 See Cassell and Walsh (1997); Kvande and Rasmussen (1995); Rothschild and Davies (1994).

2 For the German example see "Schattenbericht" on CEDAW (2003) and on Resolution 1325 (2004).

attribute to these topics but also the questionable long-term impact of such a sporadic training programme.

When a DDR programme is part of the mission's responsibilities, one of the cooperation partners is the UN Secretariat's Department for Disarmament Affairs (DDA). In 1999, DDA started to develop a gender action plan, which is the first of its kind in the UN Secretariat (Marcaillou 2003: 51). Within the organisation itself, the action plan is regarded as innovative, starting the mainstreaming process at the top of the institution itself, working its way through all hierarchical levels and into programming. An important point within the document is the acknowledgement that such a plan can merely be a starting point for a lot more lessons to be learnt and experiences to be had (DDA 2003: 1). This plan, including its top-down approach, is being replicated by other UN agencies (Heyzer 2003). Yet, as Olsson points out, the mere presence of women as well as that of a gender mainstreaming plan does not equal its implementation to the fullest potential (Olsson 2005: 179f.).

The above observations on DPKO and DDA can exemplify the situation in other agencies, developing gender mainstreaming strategies and tools. On the ground it is often an individual staff member who is appointed responsible for gender in the respective departments or units, referred to as "the gender person" (*Anna*). Despite gender mainstreaming being a "cross-cutting issue", in local implementation contexts of UN work, gender is often again "added on". This may reflect the challenges of the concept itself and the difficulties staff members entrusted with it face in a structure that is reluctant to undergo substantial changes. Puechguirbal affirms that such conditions are similar in most UN peacekeeping missions (2003b: 119).

Conclusion

Illustrated with the examination of the field of peacekeeping and disarmament, gender mainstreaming within the UN is not granted its role as an analytical tool with which to achieve goals such as gender equality and equity, as intended by the "Platform for Action". Instead, gender mainstreaming is perceived an end in itself, with the original goals forgotten or out of sight (Meintjes 2001: 74). At the same time, Abdela finds gender to be "reduced" to just the inclusion of women into programming and targeting in specific projects. Currently, this does not necessarily constitute a problem, as long as these activities do not become a substitute for the whole concept of gender mainstreaming. According to the author, such neglect of the analyses of power relations within UN structures and women's rights' issues would reduce women to instruments, tools to achieve peace, but does not include them in their own right (Abdela 2004: 99). Looking at this problem, Vincent points out that:

> [s]imply to 'include' women or women's voices [...] in a politics that is flawed and based on unsatisfactory ethical and moral bases will have little transformative effect [...] such inclusionary attempts do little more than reaffirm a "hegemonic core to which the margins are added without any significant destabilisation of that core" (Vincent 2003: 10).

With these structural challenges in mind and the potential difficulties faced by trying to implement gender mainstreaming, considering any activity or programme as "in some way 'gendered'" and fulfilling these is asking a lot from the staff involved (Mackay 2004: 107). Often, potential long-term benefits of gender mainstreaming are not understood or acknowledged in every-day work. In this notion, a lot of authors point out that practitioners doubt the necessity or (measurable) positive impact of gender mainstreaming on peace processes (Mackay 2004: 107), others acknowledge it to be there, positively influencing the stability of a post-conflict setting (Abdela 2004: 97; Olsson 2005). Whether these arguments can be enhanced and developed without running the risk of essentialising women as inherently peaceful could therefore develop into a challenging task.

In the light of the conceptual difficulties of gender's inclusion into the UN system, it appears questionable whether this can be differently achieved or even improved on the implementation level. With the example of the Sierra Leonean DDR programme, this question shall be examined in the following section.

3.2 Sierra Leone's Demobilisation process and gender mainstreaming

Demobilisation programmes as part of the transition from war to peace processes are viewed as an essential peace and confidence-building measure. As they include the disintegration of armed forces involved in the (civil) war, their procedure is highly political. Usually, warring parties take care to exert all possible influences on the proceedings and subsequent benefits as early as possible. In the case of Sierra Leone, the government had already started to plan a DDR programme as early as 1998, before the Lomé Peace Agreement was signed on 7th July 1999. The agreement reaffirms the National Committee for DDR (NCDDR) as well as the expected number of 45,000 combatants to go through DDR (Kai-Kai 2000: 114). It also calls upon the international community and the UN mission in Sierra Leone to support the programme. Peacekeepers are expected to observe and support the implementation of all stages of the programme and provide the necessary development of a secure environment. Special emphasis is laid on the disarmament component and the disbanding of "rebel fighters" which, according to Foray, distracted from the real causes of the war, calming all combatants with promises regarding the DDR programme that were impossible to fulfil in the long-run (2000: 103).

As a follow-up to the peace agreement, the UN Security Council Resolution 1270 established a corresponding mission mandate, which underlines in Paragraph 15: "the importance of including in UNAMSIL personnel with appropriate training in […] gender related provisions [and] cultural awareness" (UNSC 1999).

While the resolution does not explicitly emphasise gender mainstreaming, it acknowledges the importance of gender for a peacekeeping mission and the related work of UN agencies. Despite its limitations, with Resolution 1325 released in October 2000, the call for gender mainstreaming became even stronger. The envisioned role of women and the need for gender mainstreaming in all peace building and keeping activities of the UN are clearly outlined. Regarding DDR, special needs of female and male combatants as well as their dependents are supposed to be addressed by implementing agencies to broaden the effect of DDR as part of the peace process. As such, all DDR programmes with UN involvement should adhere to these assignments (Farr 2003b: 26).

Yet, similar difficulties as in other missions mentioned above also affected the UN mission in Sierra Leone, with little female staff in decision-making positions and virtually no female peacekeepers on the ground. As missions are evaluated according to their mandate, this would later be a point of criticism, UNAMSIL being criticised for the lack of gender-sensitivity in their work. This was mentioned in the context of internal structures, civilian affairs, but especially with regard to the DDR programme[1], for the general public the most visible part of the mission.

The Sierra Leonean DDR set-up and implementation

While UN agencies and research institutions are dealing with issues around DDR, it is usually governments in cooperation with UN missions that design and outline the process of Demobilisation for a specific country. After the Lomé agreement was signed in 1999, NCDDR coordinated the programme on behalf of the government. This organisation was structurally located within the "Commission for the Consolidation of Peace", emphasising the general wish for peace and the important role DDR should play to achieve this goal (Farr 2003b: 30).

Already at this early stage serious concerns were raised regarding the chances of integrating the former combatants into civilian life. As society and economy were partly, or in some places totally upset or destroyed by the recent war, DDR by itself could not be expected to serve both Demobilisation and reconstruction purposes (Foray 2000: 103).

Being aware of the strong political will and commitment of all parties necessary to conduct a DDR programme[2], NCDDR established institutional links to many national and international organisations to gain support for this task. The peacekeeping forces of UNAMSIL and ECOMOG, UN agencies, major donors and NGOs as well as government and commanding heads of the former fighting factions were involved (Kai-Kai 2000: 115). The organisational structure of UNAMSIL did not explicitly include the DDR Coordination Section at the beginning. Individual people who served as contact persons on DDR slowly formed a "DDR cell" which later evolved into the DDR section. Responding to current needs, less to strategic requirements and overarching goals, the UNAMSIL staff appeared to lack a conceptual background and the necessary oversight at the beginning of their task (*Dr. Kai-Kai*).

Political tensions and new outbreaks of hostilities, abduction and in some instances killing of peacekeepers and aid workers caused delays and difficulties in information acquisition and resource provision. Regarding the institutional set-up, political tensions and security concerns made it difficult

1 See Par. 20 of the Secretary-General's 21st report on UNAMSIL (UNSG 2004).
2 On this subject see Colletta et al. (1996); Kingma (2000); Knight and Özerdem (2004).

to find NGOs willing to work as implementation partners. As a consequence, problems in delivery developed, especially in regions, which were considered particularly tense (Dr. Kai-Kai). Such tensions lead to reconsiderations within the set-up. The eligibility criteria were relaxed, allowing the entry of more combatants and resulting in a major increase in the resources required. By February 2002, the disarmament and demobilisation parts were considered completed (NCDDR 2002: 4f.), with the reintegration efforts finishing in the course of 2004.

From a technical point of view, disarmament is a (military-interpreted) process of collecting, controlling and disposing of small arms and light weapons, so access to the DDR programme and associated benefits is restricted to those bearing arms (Knight and Özerdem 2004: 499). In Sierra Leone, access was at first permitted only on an individual basis, later to be changed into a group process. Combat units would appear together at the pickup points, being transported and "processed" at the disarmament site before being moved to a demobilisation camp. An essential part for the eligibility of a combatant was his or her ability to present a weapon and being identified by a commanding officer. During the encampment period health screenings were done as well as military experience recorded. Information would be given on reintegration benefits and combatants would have to make choices of communities to settle into and educational or apprenticeship programmes to partake in. At the same time, so-called "sensitisation" training on human rights, civil rights and obligations were given, supposedly preparing the former combatants for some potential challenges of resettlement into civilian life. This information is intended to secure the break-up of wartime command structures. Counselling sessions and leisure activities were planned but often not available due to restricted funding. The "encampment period" as a whole varied according to political and financial conditions of the programme. As a result, information and sensitisation could not always be provided to a sufficient extent and the social aspects of demobilisation were inhibited. Accordingly, preparations for the next step, reintegration, had only marginal impacts.

Of the about 75,000 combatants disarmed totally[1], about 71,043 were demobilised. About 56,500 people were included in vocational training,

1 The quoted numbers of participants vary: NCDDR claims 72,490, UNAMSIL DDR Section 75,468 ex-combatants (Miller et al. 2006: 14f.).

formal education or courses on agriculture with varying length from three to nine months (Molloy 2004: 7). 3,500 of the remaining so-called "case-load" without such support received a monetary "reintegration benefit" in the course of 2004 (*Dr. Kai-Kai*). The typical reintegration programme included a vocational training course in a chosen profession such as carpentry, masonry or soap making, and allowances for the time of the course as well as tool kits at the end of a course. In some places new institutions were established for this purpose, usually in urban settings, less in rural areas. Reintegration in a common sense could hardly occur due to such institutional limitations, as ex-combatants were separated from the wider communities during the course. With a regular income paid during the course, often ex-combatants were much better provided for than most other people. In some places this lead to hostilities as ex-combatants were perceived as being rewarded for their participation in the war (CVT, PRIDE).

With such economic dimensions involved, reintegration more likely occurred in "StopGap" programmes in which ex-combatants and "community youth" worked in infrastructural or recovery projects such as road, school or sanitation rehabilitation (DDR 2003a). These programmes were designed to directly and quickly benefit the hosting community and lead to closer contact of ex-combatants to the wider community. This UNDP-run activity is often considered as the real reintegration activities linked to DDR (Molloy 2004: 10).

Besides the estimated 18,000 disarmed combatants who did not take part in the whole programme, others did not even enter at all. This might be due to lack of information or active encouragement.

The numbers certainly raise the question whether all eligible participants were sufficiently targeted during the information and sensitisation phase before the actual programme had started. The Executive Secretary defended the NCDDR's focus on arms' collection and refused any additional obligations of the programme, as they were already "dealing with difficult people under difficult circumstances" (*Dr. Kai-Kai*). This, apparently, would not leave much space for targeting specific groups outside the expected category of (male) combatants.

Despite these complex conditions, one other group was included in the programme: with child soldiers in West Africa receiving a lot of media attention, the national government and UNICEF made special provisions for this group. While their actual number was more than double that expected[1], specialised agencies were contracted as IPs to assists the organisations running DDR, and with time assistance to children became an integral part of the programme (Kai-Kai 2000: 115f.).

The inclusion of children and the considerations of their specific needs reveal that with appropriate attention and interested stakeholders the Sierra Leone DDR could consider and integrate special groups quite successfully[2] (UNSG 2004). In comparison to the case of children, the "category" of women was not established and therefore no provisions were made, nor consideration given with regard to them. In the light of the gender mainstreaming obligations of the organisations involved this absence appears surprising. With the mainstreaming process supposedly securing all the possible interrelation of programmes with gender, at least indirectly women should have become an integral part of all programming, excluding all potential discrimination. How this could have happened and why it nevertheless did not happen with regard to women shall be analysed below.

Integration of women into the Demobilisation programme

While the Security Council mandate has a crucial influence on the work and potential achievements of a UN mission, the peace agreement and the decisions of the NCDDR are the key parameters along which a DDR programme can develop and evolve. The Lomé Peace Agreement does not explicitly incorporate women or women's needs into the proposed DDR programme, but it recognises their vital role in reconstructing the country, therefore calling for their integration in any related activity (Lomé Peace Agreement 1999: Article XXVIII). Within this formal recognition, women are assigned a passive, recipient role while presented as a grateful constituency for aid and development projects (Molloy 2004: 19). Regarding the actual implementation, the Executive Secretary of NCDDR, Dr. Kai-Kai outlined the organisational approach towards women. In the eyes of the commission, the programme was "gender neutral", recognising male and female combatants the same way, without any discrimination intended and possible (*Dr. Kai-Kai*).

---

1 6,787 of the demobilised combatants were under the age of 18 and therefore fell under the category child soldier (Mazurana and Carlson 2004: 2).

2 As McKay and Mazurana point out, the programme for child soldiers also lacked special attention for the concerns of girl soldiers participating in the DDR (2004: 91ff.).

With the discussion on how women could or should be integrated into DDR, the perceived purpose of the programme becomes important. DDA defines it as "to facilitate disbanding military fighters and easing their transition back into society" (DDA 2001: 1), emphasising the social and reintegration component. The Sierra Leone approach aimed at the reduction of the proliferation of SALW as well as breaking the command chains within "rebel groups" (*Dr. Kai-Kai*). It therefore concentrates on essentially military purposes and processes. With this primary aim of collecting weapons and with disarmament being the bottleneck to enter the programme, women and men were perceived as equals, able to come forward, hand in a weapon and be registered as an ex-combatant. Later, with disarmament as a group process, women could enter together with their comrades in their fighting units. No specific legitimation was necessary, except being recognised as a member of the fighting unit. Mostly, this identification was done by the respective commanding officer.

The only real women-specific activity planned was the support of (male) ex-combatants' wives in a micro-credit programme. As stated above, the political tensions and security concerns at the beginning of the DDR process limited the availability of specialised or experienced implementation partners. Those available, according to the Executive Secretary, were not willing to take up the concern of wives as they were "considered outside their mandate". Therefore, women in their roles as wives or widows could not be catered for by NCDDR as it (supposedly) lacked implementation partners "in the field" (Dr. Kai-Kai). Molloy points to the fact that agencies specialised on women were either "under-utilised or marginalized" within the mechanisms of UN and NCDDR regulations as well as strategies (2004: 16f.). Yet again it becomes obvious that within the UN system gender mainstreaming is equated with the integration of women. This attitude then has its consequences on programming even in this area.

It was only when the DDR programme was already established and running, after complaints were made, such as the XY report of the Secretary-General on the lack of "gender sensitivity" (UNSG 2004), that new steps were taken. With the term (sexual and) gender-based violence ((S)GBV)[1],

1 The interpretations and consequently acronyms may vary between "sexual" or "gender-based" violence amongst the organisations concerned, but in actual programming most of them address rape survivors. For the purpose of an all-encompassing acronym, here (S)GBV shall be used.

UN organisations and other agencies started to address survivors of rape, usually intending to target women and girls. But even in this limited understanding of gender mainstreaming, a women's rights' activist working in West African civil society stated: "Women loose out on both ends, they lose as a target group and they lose in the institutions" (*Tonieh Wiles*).

The approach taken by the Sierra Leone NCDDR holds certain challenges for women to participate in the programme, of which disarmament might be the most difficult, causing a bottleneck for women's entry in order to later receive the associated benefits. In the following section the way women as well as gender aspects were integrated into, neglected or affected by the "gender neutral" DDR process shall be examined, looking briefly at the individual programme components[1]. The points of reference are official policies and (institutional) frameworks developed by the agencies involved in the DDR, revealing gendered criteria and messages, which might be intentionally or unintentionally sent, nonetheless certainly affect women and men involved in the programme.

- Mandate

During the conception phase of the DDR, women were acknowledged as victims and perpetrators in the conflict. As such, the programme was open for them. Previous experiences show that fighting forces have between 10% and 30% women amongst their ranks (UNIFEM 2004: 12f., 31). For Sierra Leone, 12% of the originally expected 45,000 combatants were expected to be women, however the programme was only prepared for 1,000 women (*Alice*). In the light of the total number of ex-combatants nearly doubling the expectations, one can expect the difficulties encountered by all participants.

While the actual number of women who participated in the DDR remains unknown, different statistical surveys exist. Humphreys and Weinstein quote the NCDDR with 7.4% of participants being female, while they estimate their number as high as 10.9% (2004: 14). For children, other sources state the numbers for disarmament as follows: 7.7% or 529 were female (Women's Commission 2002: 4). Yet another source calculates the number of girl combatants as high as 12,056 (Mazurana and Carlson 2004: 20). Despite the diverting numbers, it becomes clear that the programme was

1 For a policy-oriented perspective on the inclusion of women combatants into DDR see UNIFEM (2004) and Watteville (2002). For women's challenges in Sierra Leone's DDR see Farr (2003b) and Mazurana and Carlson (2004).

not prepared for the large numbers of ex-combatants in general, and for the female ones in specific.

This happened despite the programme's definition of female combatants as a "vulnerable group", entitled to receive special attention (DDR 2003b: Par. 72). As this declaration appears to have been evaded, no specific targeting or sensitisation was to address and inform women. Instead, the "gender neutral" characteristic was stressed[1]. Consequently, at this stage, DDR expected women to identify simply as combatants. With the usual attributes of combatants being male, the project was designed according to these expectations (UNIFEM 2004: 4).

- Disarmament

With the emphasis on collecting weapons, the Sierra Leone disarmament process was strongly connected to the military. This image was underlined in the first phase of individual disarmament on the basis of surrendering a weapon. This was even strengthened by large groups of armed men present at the collection sites. For women to participate in DDR, they would have to identify with them in public. In Sierra Leone this included the association of shame and with no alternative category available, this was the only "identity offer" they could choose from, emphasised by the fact that they would have to either present a weapon or later come as part of a fighting unit, to be identified by the commanding officer who did not always acknowledge the combat role of the women in his unit and often took away weapons before demobilisation.

- Demobilisation

The demobilisation phase is intended to on the one hand break the "command chain", i.e. the hierarchical relationships within a fighting unit, and on the other prepare the participants for civilian life. A report of the Secretary-General summarises the aims of demobilisation as the following:

> Demobilisation refers to the process by which parties to a conflict begin to disband their military structures and combatants begin the transformation into civilian life. It generally entails registration of former combatants;

1 Staff of a local NGO suspected that this omission of women combatants was due to the restricted funding. Considering the suspected number of eligible women, their inclusion into the programme would have breached the funding (*PRIDE*).

some kind of assistance to enable them to meet their immediate needs; discharge, and transportation to their home communities (UNSG 2000).

During this time women are exposed to distinct challenges. Especially with the acceleration of demobilisation, less time and therefore less opportunity was available for forced or unwanted relationships to husbands or partners to dissolve. As ex-combatants received less information on their rights and potential future lives than originally planned, this could result in the continuation of such relationships even after DDR due to the perceived absence of alternatives (Richards et al. 2003: 50).

With the official pre-discharge orientation, special attention was given to (S)GBV, emphasising the vulnerability of women during the war. In the same notion, the entry into a fighting force, women's victimhood due to conditions and circumstances was also underlined and therefore their entry "excused" (*Elen*). On the other hand, little or no attention was paid to potentially new roles or responsibilities women took up during the war, even if this might have affected their potential for integration into a civilian life after DDR in any way. At the same time new perspectives and hopes were raised during parts of pre-discharge orientation regarding women's rights as part of civil rights, expecting vast social changes in the post-conflict society according to international regulations (*Elen*). Such information might be contrary to women's national and local rights[1] and especially life realities: "Even though there are tremendous efforts made [...] the fact remains that women still have to struggle within a macro-environment of unequal male/female power relationships" (*Alice*).

- Reintegration

Reintegration, the final step in the UN's official programme, is the longest of the three parts and also very cost-intensive. It is described as the following:

> Reintegration refers to the process which allowed ex-combatants and their families to adapt, economically and socially, to productive civilian life. It generally entails the provision of cash or in-kind compensation, training, and job- and income-generating projects (UNSG 2000).

1 For the legal situation of women in Sierra Leone see chapter 1.3.

The task of becoming a "productive" civilian poses great challenges to people who have been fighting for a long time or even grew up in war, which is the case for many young combatants after eleven years of civil war in Sierra Leone. Beyond the general fear of stigma or potential suspicion against former "rebels", men and women do face different challenges. Within the reintegration programme in Sierra Leone, gendered stereotypes were quite prevalent. With this process being equivalent to vocational training or formal education, the major offer for women was to participate in presumably appropriate courses such as hairdressing, soap making, tailoring or *gara* tie-dyeing[1], supposedly representing female occupations. Due to the lack of a job market in this area, women found it hard to find any employment after courses. Humphreys and Weinstein claim that this might also be linked to conventional expectations about women not taking part in the formal job markets (2004: 37).

The Demobilisation framework appears to have assumed women wanting to return to "home communities" and take up lives according to "traditional ideas". Support was partly given with this intention, e.g. when organising *Bundu* initiation ceremonies (*Momoh*)[2]. Such an activity clearly emphasises the intended direction of reintegration into the perceived traditional roles of Sierra Leone women. Turshen points out that this intention is apparent in most DDR processes. In her view the term "integration" instead of "reintegration" would be more appropriate to describe the designated process, as the war's experiences and effects on communities as well as individuals, including possible alterations in gender roles, would have to be taken into consideration (Turshen 2001: 91).

The expected "re-traditionalisation" of women ex-combatants after the war is underlined also by some local women's NGO's explicit exclusion of this group from their programmes, reflecting a potential stigma women face when having identified as combatants by participating in DDR. At the same time such exclusionary behaviour raises expectations of an unchallenged

1 *Gara* tie-dyeing is commonly used to summarise the local cloth processing, including different dyeing and batik techniques.

2 Initiations into *Bundu* are a rite-de-passage, suspended in many cases due to the war, but after its end quickly increasing in numbers (Coulter 2005). They are not "cleansing rituals" for combatants. These did take place in the context of *Poro* secret society, limited to male combatants (*PRIDE*). This fact is again underlining the notion of acceptability of male involvement in conflict opposed to female; see also Alden (2002: 352).

definition of women's roles in the post-conflict setting. Meintjes asserts that such processes cannot only be observed in Sierra Leone but also in other African post-conflict settings (2001: 73). Some other NGO's working with women "affected by war" do not consider them to be (ex-) combatants but victims who have been abducted and later forced into supportive roles, mainly by the RUF/SL. As such, responsibility for their deeds is taken away from the women and they are presented and addressed as victims (*Victoria Robots*; *CVT*). Considering the potential impact of organisations addressing women in a role other than victims and thereby conveying messages of empowerment or change, a male NGO-staff stated: "A woman is a woman, whatever happens. Women will not expect to change" (*CVT*).

While claiming gender neutrality, the Sierra Leone DDR programme did contain certain characteristics and programme parts that had direct gender implications or had effects along gendered lines. The short review above hints to ways in which gender perspectives were inadvertently included into the programme. At the same time it becomes clear how diverse these perspectives were, ranging from a "male-oriented" disarmament to a more "gender-ambiguous" reintegration component where traditional gender concepts are transported next to women's rights' based empowerment aspects. As such, the original gender neutrality may have led to a neglect of, and resulting from this, ambiguities in the question of gender, which in itself resulted in inconsistencies. In the chapter above, the notion was introduced that in post-conflict settings societies could be more flexible to accommodate changes. For women emerging from the war with new personal experiences in such a setting, the inconsistencies in programming could have a considerable effect on processes of (re-) integration and self-identification with regard to future lives. On this background, Meintjes claims that military- and therefore male-focussed Demobilisation altogether deprived women of any such "benefits", as programmes inadvertently tried to revert to or construct new "traditions" lacking any notion of women's empowerment (2001: 70).

Gendered identification messages obviously also affect men going through DDR. Disarmament holds ideas of male militarism regarding weapons as well as hierarchies in fighting units. As men are considered the heads of households, they are entitled to collect family provisions; financial support is calculated and distributed on this basis. The jobs offered in vocational training also enforce gendered stereotypes. Such procedures do not only reaffirm the "dominant male role" in the family or household, but also put men under pressure to be able to perform such a role and provide for a family (*Elen*). While women might experience challenges of gender roles during DDR due to incoherent treatment and information on available roles and perspectives, men's stereotypical role might be tentatively reaffirmed.

Lessons learnt from Sierra Leone? – Women in the Liberian Demobilisation programme

Liberia is experiencing a similar DDR[1] process to that in Sierra Leone. Staff and concepts have been shifted directly from Sierra Leone to Liberia. The timing[2] of the two programmes and the staff's familiarity with the region supposedly made such a shift easy. With this institutional link, expectations were high that lessons learnt from Sierra Leone would be incorporated in the Liberia programme. Regarding women in DDR, the responsible agency was UNFPA, as in Sierra Leone. With their mandate focussing on reproductive health and associated rights, their scope on women's civil rights or any empowerment work would be limited (*Maria*). Still, within the institutions pressure was exerted on a high policy level to include women into Demobilisation procedures: "[t]he thing is that they had to follow rules, so I was there at the policy level to make quite sure that they did not mainstream gender into the oblivion, which is often what happens" (*Joana Foster*).

The basis for the DDR in Liberia is the "Strategy and Implementation Framework", developed by the UN system in 2003. Having learnt from Sierra Leone Demobilisation on the criticism later voiced on the "gender neutral" programme, in this case women were explicitly included into the framework as a "vulnerable group", together with children and handicapped combatants. While stating that women's multiple roles as combatants are the basis of their vulnerability, a "network of protection and gender agencies" is called upon to provide for this group (DDRR draft 2004: 30). At the same time, a categorisation of "womenandchildren"[3] is applied throughout the draft, intending an especially sensitive approach towards and "processing" of

1 Officially, the Liberian process is called "Disarmament, Demobilisation, Rehabilitation and Reintegration Program" (DDRR). For the purpose of simplification, DDR shall remain the common acronym.

2 While the Sierra Leone DDR was declared finished in February 2004, the Liberian DDR only picked up across the whole country in June 2004.

3 For the concept of amalgamating women with children see Eade (2004: xi).

women (DDRR draft 2004: 11, 12, 41, 56). While again gender is reduced to the inclusion of women into the programme, the draft gives an impression of treating women as minors.

An advantageous change resulting from the declaration of women being a "vulnerable group" is that in comparison to the Sierra Leone DDR a more flexible access to disarmament is enabled, again the bottleneck of participating in the programme. This ease may have led to the comparative increase in the number of women entering DDR which is immediately recognisable in their participation. Already in January 2005, the number of females was as high as 24,967, or comprised of 24% of the disarmed total (NCDDRR 2005: 2).

Formally, women do not have to identify as combatants to disarm but can access in the category of "women associated with fighting forces". The intention of this broader eligibility criteria is to reduce the experience of stigma linked to being an ex-combatant for those women who wish to participate in DDR but would otherwise be repelled (UNIFEM 2004: 4). Also, some cantonment sites are reflecting specific security concerns in their set-up and specific women's needs in their equipment (UNIFEM 2004: 16). Nevertheless, disarmament and demobilisation are still an obviously military-dominated and -oriented process in which women's organisations have limited influence or access (*Roseline Toweh*; UNIFEM 2004: 19).

For reintegration, formal education and vocational training courses are prepared and implemented where possible. For the latter, UNMIL's Senior Gender Advisor aimed to make the promotion of women's participation a criterion for IPs to be contracted, even in "non-traditional trades". In her view, this was an attempt to make both an institutional for the other cooperating UN agencies, and public statement of the advancement of women after the war (*Joana Foster*).

While these points may be recognised in the sphere of the national civil society, it is questionable to what extent they can be taken up. As a women's rights' activist pointed out, the scope or potential impact of national women's organisations is contained by their limited capacities, underdeveloped due to the past war and the "patriarchal attitudes" prevailing in society (*Tonieh Wiles*). Some voices also doubt the optimistic perception voiced by the Senior Gender Advisor regarding other UN organisations. A women's rights' activist working within the system stated: "We are cut off, not only from information but also as an organisation to influence DDR on the ground" (*Anna*).

The brief reflection on the Liberian DDR process shows that despite practical changes in the interest of women, the issue of gender is again reduced to questions of integrating women. Whereas some advances have been made in comparison to the Sierra Leone framework, women's easier access to the programme is enabled by a declaration of "vulnerability", implying "special needs" as well as passiveness and victimhood. These notions are again reverting to the essentialising stereotypes discussed above.

With the continuous re-interpretation of gender mainstreaming to women's integration, issues regarding male ex-combatants' gender-related concerns, together with their exposure to militaristic processes in DDR are not yet adequately addressed either. A MilOb on his third UN peacekeeping mission observed the effect disarmament can have especially on young men after long years of fighting: "The person collapses, he becomes irritable. He is looking for guidance like a child, because he does not have the weapon any more to support him, to hold him up. This way, the men are very open to new messages" (*Robert*).

This observation hints to the missed chance of addressing challenges with male gender identities in DDR. In wartime, combatants may have acquire particular concepts of masculinity. After the conflict, the unmediated encounter with civilian concepts results in insecurity among the former combatants, leading to an increase in (domestic) violent behaviour (Molloy 2004, UNIFEM 2004). Such problems are widely observed, yet so far, within Demobilisation processes "the question of what to do with the "morass of malignant male muscle" remains unanswered" (UNIFEM 2004: 19). Sideris referred to this phenomenon as a lack of demilitarisation during Demobilisation, the programme failing to offer a non-violent "sense of manhood or masculinity" (2001: 52)[1].

In this light, the Liberian UN system reveals that gender topics and their stakeholders are still underrepresented. Despite of the Gender Unit of UNMIL being directly responsible to the head of the mission, its scope and impact is limited. When questions considering these topics are raised, one is referred to the Unit, leaving the impression that the Unit serves as an excuse for other agencies and institutions to avoid dealing with gender issues in

1 See also Flood (2005); Hearn (2001); Pease (2000).

their own work. As such, the National Commission of DDRR or UNDP Liberia do not have a gender unit or staff within their own organisations to oversee issues concerning gender in their programming. At the same time the Gender Unit is concentrating on the integration of women into the peace building processes, leaving little capacity to fulfil their original mandate of providing UNMIL staff with gender training (*Joana Foster*).

3.3 Potential effects of the Sierra Leonean DDR on gender discourses

Gender mainstreaming policies are leading to (contestable) changes in organisations' policies and working procedures. These might be inconsistent, as shown above for the Sierra Leonean DDR programme, but they still have their impact on the so-called target group of the project. How such processes can be conceptualised in the context of post-conflict situations and gender relations shall be introduced shortly.

Organisations' influences on processes of identification

As discussed above, some researchers attribute a more fluid social environment to post-conflict settings, allowing for more flexibility regarding processes of identification or gender relations. Regarding women after war, El-Bushra points out that in many instances, women face an odd situation. On the one hand their responsibilities and possibility of movement were broadened and "traditional" behavioural rules may have been challenged in everyday life during war. On the other hand social or legal dimensions are often not corresponding to these changes. This situation is analysed by some as differences on personal and broader social levels, El-Bushra referred to it as: "*De facto* gains have not been translated into *de jure* changes in women's status: women have taken on responsibility but have not been granted power" (2004: 163, emphases in original).

Taking a clearly feminist stance, the author pre-conditions that changes during war represent an improvement and women desire to expand these changes into a more general notion of empowerment. Such concepts could be supported by organisations entering the post-conflict society and implementing their projects, including specific ideas on gender. Even if they do not imply explicit ideas of empowerment, their programmes still convey gendered aspects. The DDR programme discussed above is merely one example for more or less consciously conveying messages affecting processes of identification in a post-conflict society and thereby touching the sphere of gender.

The way in which organisations and their programmes can potentially impact on social processes in a post-conflict setting and influence "alternative masculinities and femininities emerging", according to El-Bushra, needs more research (2004: 170). Therefore, as a preliminary, a study focusing on migration shall serve as a reference point. In this study, Koopmans and Statham show how institutions can influence processes of identification with people who enter a new environment via migration processes and want to claim benefits from these institutions. In the interest of gaining these benefits, people are obliged to relate to the institutions in certain, previously established categories. In this case, the state agency tries to employ already existing dimensions of identifications the migrants arrive with, which overlap, cut across or even compete with each other. With certain policies, they want to alter "the balance among diverse identifications" or even "sponsor new ones" to foster changes in migrants' behaviour or attitudes. The authors assert that this is by far not an overt process, but takes subtle forms:

> By sponsoring and rewarding some of these [...] identities, and discouraging others, receiving states might alter the balance among such multiple identities and switch migrants' primary alliances (Koopmans and Statham 2001: 13).

While the authors use a narrowed one-way process of influence, easing the analysis but limiting the potential understanding of multiple interrelationships of institutions and their target groups, the study gives an impression of how intricately influences of identification can be interwoven with claims-making procedures. In the long run, the authors find that migrants at least publicly adhere to the "offered" categories, and that over time this influences people's self-perceptions and personal identification processes.

Transferred into the present context, the study describes the influences agencies' categorisations of target groups may take on processes of people's identification in a post-conflict setting. Regarding aid or refugee projects, similar developments have been analysed for their impact on gender roles (Meintjes et al. 2001). With NGO programmes of women's empowerment through broadened economic responsibilities, El-Bushra shows that parts of the population link such processes to resulting cultural changes and attribute blame directly to the NGOs. If women used the newly accessible power or influence in their own interest, this was perceived as breaching traditional ideas of women's behavioural norms (El-Bushra 2004: 162, 165f.).

Applied on the effect organisations can have by offering identification, especially if they include certain benefits, gender dimensions in DDR will have their effect on people participating in (or opting out of) the processes. Whether consciously employed like in Koopmans' and Statham's study or indirectly used as a tool like in El-Bushra's discussion of the refugee context, the ambiguous and sometimes inadvertent understanding and interpretation of gender within the Sierra Leonean DDR has certainly had an effect on is participants. These could be achieved by emphasising certain characteristics in their involvement in the war, offering benefits like money or taking part in skills training projects by identifying with concepts of ex-combatant. Receiving information on potential difficulties of entering civilian life or being treated as a victim of war's circumstances all offer ways in which this influence could be exerted.

Gendered contents within the Demobilisation programme

Despite the wide acknowledgement of women participating in combat and war, the essentialised image of women is still a peaceful one. Their important role in peace building and consolidation is widely recognised, yet implemented on an insignificant level regarding actual participation in peace negotiations or any other high-profile peace building activity (Farr 2003b: 30). They are usually considered and mentioned as holding social capital for the reintegration of (supposedly male) combatants or refugees and in this framework they should be supported (Turshen 2001: 89f.).

Expressing an idea that accords with the wider institutional attitude, the Sierra Leone DDR Section Officer in Charge points out how women are to be included into Disarmament consideration and programmes due to their knowledge of weapon storage or hiding places and the potential influence they can exert on "their men" to disarm and integrate into civilian life (Molloy 2004). Women are to be included due to their (expected) positive effects on peace processes, supporting community security and national reconciliation. This attitude remains in the essentialistic perspective on women and reveals lack of gender sensitivity as well as failing to respect women as having equal rights in the decision-making processes of their lives. Women in their "passive" and "peace-supporting" role have even experienced direct and overt instrumentalisation by DDR planners of civil society: "The community leaders undertook to provide land for ex-combatants to farm and build homes, and wives for them to marry and start families" (Foray 2000: 106, emphases added).

Besides objectification of women, these concepts even reveal lack of institutional will to overcome gender stereotypes and adhere to the requirements of gender mainstreaming. On this background, Farr points out that the (relatively new) emphasis on "the civilian woman" in peace processes discloses the perpetuated difficulty of conceptualising and working with women in their non-stereotypical roles as combatants (Farr 2003b: 27). This underlines Väyrynen's observation (2004) that the UN, in their peace and conflict work, are still caught up in dichotomising perspectives, in this case with regard to women and men as well as gender roles. While the inclusion of women in general is a favourable development, it should not be limited to the "peaceful" ones or distract from those women who were, to whatever extent, participating in armed conflict. At the same time, their inclusion must not lead to instrumentalisation or objectification.

The above observations reveal that UN and their programmes are indeed working with ideas of gender roles, be it the intentional or mere side affects, despite or exactly because the UN system reduces gender mainstreaming to the question of including women. With the different aspects of DDR and the various messages it conveys on potential (gender) roles in conflict and post-conflict settings, participating agencies are sometimes emphasising passive female victims, sometimes expecting women combatants to identify with militarised and male-connoted roles. While no systematic reflection is being done on the war's effect on gender roles, in some reintegration projects it is assumed that women would want to take up "non-traditional trades" due to the new or broadened tasks they managed during the war. At the same time other reintegration measures facilitated the presumed re-integration into traditionally influenced "home communities". These activities are taking place on the background of women's unspecified social standing in the war environment, upsetting behavioural norms regarding women's status and respectability (Molloy 2004: 18). The DDR programme, the IPs and the comparatively ill-considered gender policies within the UN system are certainly contributing to these ambiguities.

Molloy claims that by DDR "failing women" the programme did not have lasting effects on their lives. However due to the supposedly inadvertent messages on (gender) identities, it might affect their lives in a long-term perspective by contributing to discourses on identity and gender taking place in wider society. Therefore, a "gender-neutral" programme does have an effect, if only by automatically disadvantaging women in participation and its associated benefits (DDA 2001: 1; Hale 2001).

In the general context of war and social change, agencies acknowledge the potential empowerment women might experience by being exposed to extreme situations with new challenges (Meintjes et al. 2001: 15). Nevertheless, how these changes can or should be perpetuated is controversial. The UNIFEM DDR handbook proposes that without outside support, the desired changes, having been started in the war, need outside support to overcome the "inescapable re-traditionalisation" of post-conflict societies (UNIFEM 2004: 39). Opposing this, Meintjes points out that such a support cannot be imported from the outside but has to be generated from within the society by women who are organised in institutions and willing to speak up for themselves and champion their rights (Meintjes 2001: 76).

While such discussion may give the impression of war having some positive effects for women, offering new identity options and the prospect for empowerment, the incredible amount of suffering implied in war should not be forgotten. Yet, this perspective should not hinder the view of coping strategies being developed, survival secured and agencies being used during these dire times. In this vein, the following chapter examines women's perspectives and agencies in their reactions to the DDR programme, revealing their choices and active engagement with the process.

4 Women engaging with the gender mainstreaming efforts

Women's engagements with the Sierra Leone DDR programme did not occur in an isolated atmosphere but were part of discourses taking place in the wider post-conflict setting. These are influenced by organisations and institutions making their impact on identification processes by offering projects and benefits to specific groups of people who fit into the programme categories and thereby become the designated "target group".

Koopmans' and Statham's study on institutions' influence on identifications in claims' making processes shall be used as a reference point for the analysis of identification relating to women and gender issues as they were included in the Sierra Leone DDR programme. The following chapter examines the effects that introduced or reinforced categories of identification have on those women potentially constituting a target group of Demobilisation. These are women who have lived through and participated in the war, with the research focussing on those who experienced the conflict in the more rural parts of Eastern Sierra Leone and later faced DDR activities in and around the towns of this area. While they did not necessarily participate in it, they certainly interacted with the concepts and ideas presented, upon which some women combatants decided to take part in other projects. Some of them are related to Demobilisation, others are institutionally independent but work to support those women "left out" of the DDR.

The strategies women employ facing the ascribed, assigned or designated characteristics of identification or certain roles in society will be examined more closely. These investigations will be are based on experiences and observations of Sierra Leonean women and men as well as local NGO staff. By doing so, the effects the conveyed identification messages have on gender roles, women's self-images and post-conflict discourse in the wider society shall be reflected upon.

4.1 Consequences of gender mainstreaming: Women entering or opting out of DDR

> Disarmament that focuses only on utilising civilians marginalizes another group of women – those who fought in armed combat and voluntarily or forcibly supported combatants as nurses, cooks or sex-workers. […] [P]recisely because it does not fit social stereotypes of what makes a 'good woman', [this group] attracts the greatest social opprobrium in the reintegration and reconstruction period (Farr 2003b: 29f.).

Farr describes the situation of many women in Sierra Leone who fulfilling overlapping tasks of combat and service provision, otherwise attributed to so-called "camp followers". These experiances may breach social expectations and roles otherwise available to women. They may therefore experience more difficulties with entering the post-conflict setting than others, as they had "occupied multiple spaces and identities" during the war which later need mediation to make sense of them (Farr 2003b: 29). Most DDR programmes appear to be inappropriate in addressing and incorporating these diversities and thereby end up "ignoring" women (Puechguirbal 2003a: 24).

Choices: Entering Demobilisation

> We only looked after people who came forward; we did not go looking out for more (*Dr. Kai-Kai*).

Without special sensitisation or addressing of women to enter disarmament, women had to use their own initiative and try to enter the process. Both in the early individual and the later group disarmament women were confronted with specific challenges. Often, commanding officers took away guns that would have made the women combatants eligible to join the programme, thus preventing their entry. Some perceived women as not entitled to enter and wanted them to remain in their supporting role, in the background (*Foday Sajuma*). In a group discussion in Kailahun, young women repeatedly pointed out that they were not welcomed by their immediate male comrades to join the process, but were instead told: "Go after your child!" (*CASTC*). To be equated with children and reminded of women's "household chores" was a widely shared experience of women who wanted to disarm

(*FAWE Koidu* and *Yengema*). Such statements underline the perception of male comrades or commanders that women were not eligible to enter as only genuine fighters were supposed to participate: “The men will just see you [a woman combatant] as girlfriend, themselves as husbands. That’s why if you ask them how many female combatants were there, they cannot tell, because they don’t recognise them as combatants” (*PRIDE*).

Like Farr stated above, the multiple and intersecting roles taken up by women during the war[1] lead them to be conceptually located within established roles, during and also after fighting. Consequently, their activities as combatants are not recognised as equal to the more “traditional” work they also performed.

For women to enter the DDR process, they would have to overcome the identification as a “camp follower” and identify clearly as a combatant to then face the military process of disarmament. With peacekeepers securing the site and MilObs conducting the interviews, disarmament and demobilisation have a military face, despite an overall de-militarisation of the combatants being intended. A woman working in DDR for a local NGO observed that a lot of women combatants felt uncomfortable in the presence of so many armed and uniformed men, additional to the comrades of their fighting unit. Previous trauma inflicted by combat, torture or rape during war would surface again:

> We are trying to de-traumatise them [women ex-combatants] from the uniforms but with the MilObs and peacekeepers in their uniforms, they are still present at the demob[ilisation] site. So we don’t usually associate with the MilObs to do our work (*Kariatu*).

Aside of the necessity to secure the disarmament and demobilisation sites, the UN is perceived as giving a military impression of DDR, with only armed combatants being eligible for the process. Making group disarmament a requirement later reinforced this impression. Here, a commanding officer had to be present and identify each combatant as belonging to his fighting unit. Therefore, with women not being identified as genuine fighters, their chances to enter were even more diminished as now a commander’s identification became more important than the previous criteria, the ability to hand over a gun.

1 For an exemplary breakdown of women’s tasks see chapter 1.3.

After women managed to enter the first phase of DDR, they appear to be more affected by wartime incidents upon which they prefer to leave the programme (Watteville 2002). A woman who had started the reintegration programme after managing to pass through disarmament and demobilisation explained her reasons for opting out of the programme. In the vocational training course she was faced with a person who had raped her during the war:

> Then I join in NCDDR and see the perpetrator. I have to leave. I cannot finish the programme. I go away from the training cause I can't look at him or be in the same room with him. I have not forgotten what he did to me (*female ex-combatant, CVT*).

After the terrible events during the war, avoiding the presence of the man who inflicted violence on her was so important to this woman that she preferred to discontinue the training and thereby give up the regular income which would have secured her and her child's livelihood for the time of the course. Just like this case, personal experiences acted as deterrents to many other women who wished to participate in courses of the reintegration programme or even earlier, during the encampment phase of demobilisation. A staff member of an INGO offering skill's training for ex-combatants observed that confrontations with perpetrators of sexual or gender-based violence were a significant cause of women withdrawing from the programme. Amongst men, in comparison, perpetrated violence mostly lacked this sexual nature and therefore enabled an interaction less connected with shame and morality (*Alice*). One other reason to opt out of the programme was the fact that training courses were often held at specially established institutions, in some places known as "the combatants' place". Being seen there would reinforce the need to constantly publicly identify as a combatant, even if these women were trying to blend into a community.

Overall, the system of DDR did not leave much space for negotiating participation, with the entry being limited to those presenting arms or being identified as a combatant by others and by oneself. With the potential identification as a combatant from the outside being hard to avoid, the scope of women's choices to enter Demobilisation at all may appear questionable. The importance of self-identification in this context is examined below. This shall contribute to the understanding of how interrelated factors, among them roles perceived as traditional, could influence this process.

Choices: Deciding against Demobilisation

> At that time, during fighting, tradition was nowhere. But now, people have come back. They have started doing what they used to do. So you see, seeing a woman at that time, it was lawlessness, anybody could do anything. But today, a woman should not do such things. (*male ex-combatant, CVT*).

While some women had difficulties entering the DDR process, others did not endeavour to do so. There are versatile reasons for this, many of them involving fear of acquiring a stigma related to being an ex-combatant, having breached social norms and committed atrocities. For women, many interviewees affirmed that such an association would be "untraditional" or "shameful"[1]. Women also face allegations of impurity more than men. Additionally, cleansing rituals were sometimes available but participation was limited to men (Eno in Bop 2001: 29). In the Eastern part of Sierra Leone ex-combatants have to face allegations of being rebels[2] unless they were members of the CDF. With the ritual and spiritual links to *Poro*, the local factions of the CDF officially did not have women amongst their ranks[3]. Therefore, any women identifying as ex-combatant has to face a "double stigma" of having fought and of being a rebel (*CVT*). As a consequence, women were observed to withhold from the Demobilisation process.

Some women were warned, as in the case indicated below, about the potential consequences of their participation in DDR: "I was told by my family: 'That was the war, that was the past; let's forget about that. Do not go to disarm!'" (*woman ex-combatant, CVT*).

Associations with the Demobilisation programme would only have verified the already stigmatising connection to combat and may have lowered the chances of a woman being received back into her community. Commu-

1 Sierra Leone is no exception in this; see Afshar and Eade (2004) or Meintjes et al. (2001) for examples from other conflict areas.

2 The term "rebel" is now used mainly in the context of the RUF/SL, one of the loosing parties of the civil war, which had had its stronghold in the Eastern and Southern parts of the country.

3 Researchers widely contest this official stance; see amongst others Humphreys and Weinstein (2004); Mazurana and Carlson (2004); Richards et al. (2004).

nity acceptance depended not only on the support of immediate family but also on that of the chief. In this context, Shaw points to an understanding of reintegration among the *Temne* and other groups in Sierra Leone working through public forgetting of war-related deeds. By not "pulling it outside" of the family home, the risk of "endowing it with reality" should be evaded (Shaw 2005: 9). In this sense, entering DDR would not allow forgetting; instead it would perpetuate remembering and therefore inhibit reintegration and social healing. Due to the understanding that tradition or shared norms regulate women's behaviour more strongly, the call for women to adhere to these norms would be stronger than for men.

In some locations, women's opting out of the Demobilisation process is interpreted as "being shy", a characteristic generally ascribed to women in Sierra Leone, as a female staff of a (S)GBV programme pointed out:

> To imagine women to be fighters, they would look at them, it's just as if they had been stigmatised. A lot of them *shy away* from this thing [DDR] […] They fear the implications. So most of them didn't come out at all to admit that they have been fighting (*Victoria Robots*, emphasis added).

This perspective was often shared by people or organisations working with ex-combatants (e.g. PRIDE, MOCKY). As such, women not entering DDR seemed to fulfil expectations based on gender stereotypes, "being shy", opting, in UN terminology, for "self-demobilisation".

For this process, they chose to identify in another way, implying a different explanation of their lives during war. They associated with the fate of many women who had been abducted by the factions and had then been forced to perform duties, later labelled as "camp followers", "bush wives" or even "sex slaves" by international aid agencies (HRW 2003; PHR 2002). Observing the overlapping of tasks and duties in the camps, this choice of self-identification was an accessible and credible one, but still implying a choice consciously taken by many women. This way, chances of being identified as an ex-combatant and potential rebel were lower. Nevertheless, many women faced additional challenges resulting from rape or unapproved relationships, especially if they emerged from the war with children from these encounters.

4.2 Gendered categories: Victimisation as self-protection or lack of agency

With the DDR having no consistent gender concept and therefore giving ambiguous impressions and supporting different gender stereotypes, women facing the programme found themselves with limited options. On the one hand, they could enter and comply with characteristics of a (male-associated) combatant and thereby hope to be accepted as eligible, or they could identify as abducted and by this hope to gain access to respective projects. These two choices could be considered binary oppositions on a scale of multiple, diverse and interdependent options of taking up roles, affecting the processes of identification in the post-war situation. As Farr points out above, DDR and with it much of the post-conflict discourse do not recognise the full scale of women's potential overlapping roles and experiences during the war, but limit themselves to these comparatively "clear-cut" positions (2002: 6; see also 2003a, 2003b). These may be partially supported and encouraged by various social mechanisms such as forgetting as an instrument of social healing (Shaw 2005); nonetheless they also take their effect on the women they are trying to address.

This institutional "dichotomisation" of women is interdependent with public opinions on the potential roles of women during the war. They reveal a clear division into perpetrators and victims and do not leave much flexibility for the negotiation of wartime roles:

> There were some women [in the RUF] who have never fought in the war – they took part in the [military] training, but never fought. Some people, who have been abducted and did not do any harm to people, they are victims. So there are two types of people: perpetrators and victims (*female ex-combatant, CVT*).

The "bush wife complex" – an institutionalised category

During the war in Sierra Leone, a lot of women had been abducted and taken as so-called "forced wives" or "sex slaves". While such fates had been extensively described by INGOs and in the immediate official post-war discourse (HRW 2003; PHR 2002), it is not a topic commonly referred to by women themselves. Sexual abuses and their consequences tend to be treated with discretion and in private. The terms "bush wives" and "bush marriages" feature more openly in the debate on women and their war experiences. They relate the origin of the marriage from "the bush", the "uncivilised" or "unregulated" (Ferme 2001) and imply rebel associations (Richards et al. 2003: 14ff.). They also hold implications of rape and associated shame. The fact that these relationships had not been appropriately sanctioned and are therefore often considered un-approvable, affects power relationships within the "marriage":

> We take a man, and he was with a woman and he will want to return to the community. It would be a lot easier for the man to return now with his wife, not with any woman, right [...] He can leave her easily. But for his wife, it would be almost impossible to do the same to a wife (*PRIDE*).

In more established circumstances marriages are guarded by the wife's maternal uncle who could intervene in cases of the wife's maltreatment or represent her in divorce negotiations. However, un-sanctioned wartime 'bush' marriages did not normally enjoy such protections (Richards et al. 2004: 3). Critics therefore point to a danger of "institutionalising" these relationships:

> We shouldn't look at them just as 'bush wives'. I wouldn't want to use that term, course in the end they institutionalise the 'bush wives', you know. You have to work around that, these are wives of soldiers and they should be regarded as such. They should be able to say: 'We are soldiers and this is my wife, this is my family!' (*Tonieh Wiles*).

Even though they are not sanctioned and therefore imply potential negative consequences, a lot of these relationships are still being upheld[1].

Despite the negative connotations, a lot of women identify as "bush wives". While providing some protection from allegations of combat participation, the categorisation as "bush wife" allows some kind of identification related to an established system of reference, emphasising the lives and roles taken up during war aside from combat. Simultaneously, women identifying as "bush wives" are eligible to participate in special programmes and associ-

1 See Richards et al. (2003) for more details on legal and economic abuse of women who are regarded as "bush wives".

ated benefits. These programmes made the concept known and at the same time attractive to identify with.

Organisations encouraging women's victimhood and gender equality

Many women turned to the option of "bush wife"-identification to claim benefits and to evade the otherwise male-constructed ex-combatant and rebel stigma. This kind of identification was confirmed and even promoted in some projects. These usually aimed at supporting women, less so than at ex-combatants who had participated in DDR and were now taking part in a reintegration project, but more as partners or widows of (ex-) combatants, of whom many identified as "bush wives". In some parts of Sierra Leone, NCDDR implemented micro-credit schemes to support ex-combatants' wives, in this case even officially termed "bush wives" (*Dr. Kai-Kai*). This programme was introduced to alleviate the pressure on Demobilisation for not providing any support to the women who were part of fighting units but were not eligible, willing or able to enter Demobilisation (*Dr. Kai-Kai*; *PRIDE*).

A different way for NGOs to address women is via projects employing the concept of (sexual and) gender-based violence. This term features in many NGO programmes wanting to "target" women. Because wartime rape had already been widely acknowledged, it enabled organisations to address women without any specification of ex-combatant or "bush wife". But (S)GBV again emphasises women's vulnerability and victimhood. As such, their assigned roles in many project environments are quite clear:

> [M]ost times we pity them. I think what brought about the war, they are not responsible […] they were victims of the circumstances that lead to the war. So we say, they are as if they are children that belong to this country, children who have problems (*Victoria Robots*).

The association with children, as discussed above, is quite common in the general (post-) war atmosphere, as well as in particular projects, trying to emphasise the perception of an unaccountable and passive role women were perceived to have had in entering the war. The status of victims also fits the wider public perception:

> Women fighting in the war, they were a big group. But it is culturally not accepted, even if people know they fought. Some of them were abducted, some of them were drugged, they did not participate out of free will (*local male NGO staff, CVT*).

Parallel to the acknowledgement of women fighting in the war, the assertion of their victimhood, having been abducted or drugged, serves as an apologetic explanation. This admissible possibility reveals the perceived strength of cultural norms, according to which women should have never taken up such activities. Their potentially voluntary entrance and participation in war is not even a recognisable option[1]. Sideris points out that the perception of women's victimisation, even in combatant roles, happens according to a similar general perception of women as rather passive and peaceful, usually only the victims of any kind of violence. According to the author, this notion is employed by the particular women themselves or by other people, including women in the wider society (Sideris 2001: 49).

The "option" given by the organisations to women to identify as a "bush wive" corresponds to the more traditional expectations of women's roles. The potential resulting impression was that DDR and related programmes were encouraging a "(re-) traditionalisation" of those women involved in the war. Yet, as Thompson and Eade point out, this perspective cannot be limited to mere victimisation; instead, references to tradition are in many instances also used as a protection, during the war and, in this case, also after the war (2004: 233). As a consequence, identifying as a "bush wife" does not automatically fulfil the passive picture of oppression but implies the weighing of options and related benefits included in the category. While Moser and Clark point out that by viewing people as victims their agencies would be inhibited (2001a: 4), in this case "bush wife" appears to imply active choices and does not exclude agency per se.

The option of taking up the role of a victim of war's circumstances provides female ex-combatants with an available alternative to male-associated ex-combatants or to trying to fade back into civilian life without the otherwise associated attention. However for some women it holds limitations concerning their individual processes of identification. Hawa, a woman ex-combatant participating in a reintegration project, expresses this dilemma:

---

1 For examples of voluntary mobilisation see Peters and Richards (1998) or Richards et al. (2003).

> They [DDR project staff] talk to me like a kid at home, like one of their own children. But they don't remember my own children, that I was a wife [...] They do not talk to me about the war and what happened to me there and what I did there (*Hawa Sheriff*).

Hawa finds herself on the one hand enjoying the comfort and support of the project environment, without being accused for the past. On the other hand, she does not feel acknowledged as an adult, as a mother or as an ex-combatant and war-widow. These other aspects of personal history and experience, shaping not only memory but also perspectives for the future, remain untouched or undervalued in connection to a victim's role. The multiple and intricate interrelationships of roles are not being acknowledged to the full extent when focussing on women's victim role in a project, even if this holds protective and supportive aspects.

The advantage of the "bush wife complex" is that it is comparatively easily accessible and more readily recognised by the wider community, with NGOs and other institutions taking part in shaping these options. Simultaneously, many other roles taken up during war are faded out to fit the category of victim or "bush wife". Considering the concepts of secrecy for the purpose of social healing, strategies such as these are consistent with other local practices. Yet, it is questionable whether these omissions happen consciously on the side of the organisation and on that of the women and how their interaction would be different if also other roles were acknowledged in the project work.

In demobilisation and in some reintegration programmes, different expectations were raised about women's options after the war, this being a reflection of the inconsistent gender policies within DDR. Civil and women's rights' "sensitisation" as part of the demobilisation programme were sometimes well received and raised expectations for substantial changes of women's lives after the war:

> The women appreciate the knowledge of what are their rights and all the things concerning (S)GBV, especially when they come out of a culture of silence, such as here. So they know their rights and they want to claim them now – after all, they fought for change. But we [NGO staff] have to tell them that they have to wait till society changes as well, till all the people understand that the change is good and necessary. But some of them don't want to wait (*Elen*).

With such programmes hopes are being raised about the changes and potential achievements that the war had brought about in a general political sense and especially concerning women's rights. At the same time, Elen observes that such information may even encourage the existing and, to a degree unrealistic high hopes held by women ex-combatants. Therefore she cautions them not to be disappointed when entering civilian life. While implying even women's empowerment issues in their work, some organisations are already concerned about the impact these messages might have. The information given on women's rights is based on international legal standards and does not necessarily match the reality of local lives in a lot of instances. Being aware of this problem, Elen maintains that the changes suggested in their work are "good and necessary", taking a clear (personal) stance on women's empowerment. At the same time she does not see a strategy available to NGOs to foster the desired change in the post-conflict setting, but feels wary of letting the women ex-combatants know the limited hope she personally has for substantial changes in gender relations (*Elen*).

A formerly high-ranking RUF/SL member, Ms. Ngombeh, has a slightly different perspective on the role Demobilisation and ex-combatants should have played after the war:

> Women used to follow the men to the front line. But now, they don't do nothing. They did not keep their strength, because they were not educated enough in the DDR. If they were educated in their rights, they would still continue to work hard for women's empowerment […] Women changed during the war, but now they need encouragement (*Jamba Ngombeh*).

Ms. Ngombeh asserts that traditional gender roles were challenged and women's self-perception changed during the war, just like the NGO staff cited above. Furthermore, from her perspective, outside influence should have supported and therefore stabilised these changes. Her statement underlines the perception that war took its influences on female gender roles and that, as a consequence, women ex-combatants should act as "agents of change", pushing for the cause of women's empowerment. To be able to use the "window of opportunity", women would need the encouragement of civil society. Obviously, the victim-based "bush wife complex" a lot of organisations have introduced hampers the chances to do so. Instead of supporting supposed changes of gender roles, they would support a more conservative trait, pushing the women back into "traditional" roles instead of "empowering" them (*Jamba Ngombeh*).

With her comments, Ms. Ngombeh is representing the perspective of many women who belong to the formally educated, urban strata of the (mainly Freetown-based) elite. Organised in campaigns such as the "50/50 Group" they are pushing for the use of the "window of opportunity", aiming for a leap in women's rights and empowerment after the war. Hale underlines this point that women belonging to the elite of a movement or country would regard female war participants identifying in any other way than ex-combatants as "backward" and obstructing the desired change, without considering the effects such decisions might have on the individual lives of these less privileged women (2001: 133).

Public perception of organisations influencing female ex-combatants

The post-war period in Sierra Leone is generally associated with change, even if the kind or direction is not necessarily specified. While change and development are sometimes constructed opposite to tradition, in the current circumstances, there are intricate perceptions. As related in chapter 2, war and mobilisation in its cause are integral parts of society and therefore engaging with its aftermath is also regulated by social conventions. In this context the local perception often voiced is that the war was a deviation or rupture of ordered every-day-life, change and healing might therefore happen by returning to "traditional" life:

> So basically, even though there were breakdowns of norms, values and traditions during the war, now that the war is over, I think that we should go back, we should maintain our culture, traditions and customs. We should not forget about them, not throw them away, continue our female initiation, our male dominant role, those kinds of things. People still want to live like this (*local male social worker, CVT*).

While this statement expresses the desire of returning to tradition and culture, it already implies that they are being contested. Endorsing this, conference participants from Sierra Leone give an impression concerning the prospects of women after the civil war: "Nothing of the old structure exists;

there isn't anything to go back to which will give you that [traditional] identity" (cited in Turshen 2001: 82).

These voices perceive women unable to return to or re-enter "traditional" identification processes in the face of war's vast destructive impact on Sierra Leonean society. If women could not do so, they would have to establish new ideas. In the light of the discussion on women's roles being immersed and integral part of collective identity processes, a challenge of the old roles or an establishment of new ones would lead to substantial upheaval of perceived social norms. Thus, it is only consistent to put the development of women's identification processes and social control in the post-conflict setting under close observation.

Such discourses are not isolated from the influence of (international) organisations, introducing their attitudes and perspectives in their programming. Alongside the ex-combatants receiving information and so-called "sensitisation" regarding women's rights, the general public is also included in the course of post-war reconstruction projects. Information was given on a general level regarding political involvement of women in the local elections of 2004. These campaigns were aimed at the participation of women in the election process, casting their votes as well as becoming candidates for the newly established municipal councils. Most of these messages were based on an approach of women's equal rights.

In those areas where reintegration projects of the DDR were taking place, special information was trying to prepare the population for ex-combatants on whose behaviour and interaction the war would have taken its affects. In a small town with a high concentration of skills-training projects for this group, a community elder related her impression of the information given on the subject:

> Now, after the war, women have the right to do anything, to feed their own children, to do anything, we heard this in the talks on 50/50[1]. We women were punished in the war, men were then strong. But now, women are

1 Using the term "50/50" for issues relating to gender equality reveals the great impact of the local NGO "50/50 Group", promoting women's rights and their participation in politics. The group's campaign was widely recognised and made such a great impact that their name became synonymous for gender equality.

> getting stronger *small small*. I like that. We women should be proud of what we do, what we achieve. Then we will be strong, we will be happy (*Fatmata Abu*).

Ms. Abu depicts the rights-based approach a lot of the organisations are using and also highlights the positive effects that the women should enjoy in the future. Her comments also suggest that, having experienced the war, women were changing and "getting stronger". Given the impossibility of returning to pre-conflict conditions and the effect the war is perceived to have had on women, she perceives a need to adjust to the changes. The information and ideas women's organisations include in their work enter into this discourse and may raise concerns:

> That [accommodating changes of gender roles] is really the challenge. Women are thinking now. Some still hold the traditional belief that they are subject to men. But some do believe that: 'Oh, I can do what the man can do!' So some women are thinking differently, and some are trying to maintain their cultural beliefs (*male ex-combatant*, *CVT*).

At the same time as pointing out the changes that are apparent in women's behaviour, diversity in women's reactions to these changes is also acknowledged. Yet, a clear value is also linked to these developments, favouring the maintenance of "cultural believes".

Besides their individual attitudes on desirability, these statements are conceding the inevitability of contestation or challenge regarding women's roles after the war. In most comments potential changes are attributed to a combination of the impact war and the programmes concerning gender equality or "50/50".

While various organisations give different information on the subject of women's rights or empowerment, not all of them appear to be received and engaged with to the same extent. Along with Ms. Ngombeh, PRIDE therefore points to the need of intensifying and at the same time broadening the programmes to include more practical aspects:

> For now, I think, it would do very well if the action followed [concerning women's rights] and this information went where the situation is very difficult for people. We have to think how to get it to the people, so that women can accept it, too. Cause some are totally against 50/50, especially

> with regard to women in politics. But for women, some women will take this 50/50 idea and say no, but for women's human rights, they will make more noise (*male ex-combatant and founding member of PRIDE*).

In this statement, limitations of such programmes are addressed, regarding their scope but also content. While some dimensions of women's empowerment appear desirable and acceptable, others do less. As a result, women's reactions to an all-encompassing call for equality vary.

The above perspectives point to a discourse underway in the wider Sierra Leone society on how to react and maybe incorporate the many programmes concerning women and also potentially associated incentives. One of the biggest enticements is the widely promoted link of "the West [having] development because they have gender equality" (*Elisabeth Gbah*). With this argument it is regarded as possible to induce the ideas of gender equality due to the fact that development in an economic sense is widely desired. That such a manoeuvre is necessary reveals the (fear of) contestation of gender equality and the perceived difficulties in conveying it by other means.

As the discourse proceeds, the degree to which people feel they can accept changes is variable. Reactions to specific modifications in gender roles are quite diverse. Obviously people make choices and some are more ready to accept certain kinds of change than others. With desires to return to or maintain an earlier perception of culture but at the same time accepting differences to "tradition" that hold the promises of development, people appear willing to accommodate selected alterations.

On this background the perceptions of women ex-combatants are varied with a lot of the discourse introduced above manifesting itself in their persons. While it is commonly known that categories of "bush wives" and women ex-combatants are not clearly differentiable and a large proportion of women would rather fit into both categories than just one, officially the divide is upheld. This implies that the public preference lies on the victim category, termed above the "bush wife complex", whereas an "ex-combatant complex" would hold certain negative associations that clearly do not fit with the partially desired continuation of traditional beliefs. Women who identify with the latter are perceived to breach norms they should otherwise adhere to after the war, after the return to "normal" life. Every-day contraventions often mentioned in context with women ex-combatants were smoking cigarettes or *ganja* in public, behaving loudly and not being submissive in cases of disagreements or not obeying people perceived to be senior to them. In this aspect, some women appear to envy these female ex-combatants to some extent for the comparative "freedom" they are seen to be claiming for themselves: "During fighting, they got used to a free life" (*Mbalu*). Yet simultaneously, Mbalu expresses how inappropriate or impossible the perpetuation of such "freedom" would be.

If faced with a conflict, women ex-combatants are said to become aggressive and fight more easily, a behaviour certainly not fit for any woman, whatever her role in society may be (*Mbalu*).

Women ex-combatants are also associated with the increasing commercial sex work: "All these women [ex-combatants] on the streets, they are left there from the war and now they are destroying the morale in our communities" (*Abu Musa*).

Not wanting to integrate into the community, women ex-combatants are said to "choose" the "life on the street" in the major towns and earn a living as prostitutes (Richards et al. 2003: 15). In Mbalu's perspective on freedom from the usual subservient behaviour expected from women, this would be an option for escaping the submissive position which women are otherwise expected to uphold.

The various associations, organisations or programmes supporting the ex-combatant identity are said to "raise eyebrows", meaning they are perceived to be inhibiting the integration of the ex-combatant women. This is due to the assumption that they encourage the continuation of the problematic behaviour these women are supposed to be displaying. Despite acknowledging change, also regarding women's rights, women ex-combatants are still expected to adhere to accepted behaviour patterns. There is a feeling that they should not be encouraged to maintain their war-related identities and associated behaviour. Instead they are expected to leave these behind and adhere to more conventional, that is traditional, ways of behaviour.

As such, organisations are perceived to directly influence the reintegration of women previously involved in war, but often in a negative sense, supporting these women so they can maintain negative characteristics that they took up during the conflict. A deeper discourse on substantial changes of gender roles during the war hardly occurs. In this situation the ideas voiced on gender equality are not opposing the impression that changes regarding women's rights and equality are happening or are even desirable and necessary for the development of the country. But they point to the limits of the acceptable extent of these changes or the reluctance to face the war's potential impact on people's identities.

4.3 Women ex-combatants' agency: Options of identification

> The notion of agency attributes to the individual actor the capacity to process social experiences and to devise ways of coping with life, even under the most extreme forms of coercion. Within the limits of information, uncertainty and other constraints that exist, social actors are 'knowledgeable' and 'capable' (Long, cited in Moser and Clark 2001a: 4f.).

Long's perspective on agency focuses on acquirable qualities, that is know ledge and capability, which make people into social actors equipped with their individual agencies. Though employing this approach focuses on the options and choices available to people, it should not diminish or divert from the dire conditions people live in after the war. Instead, the approach aims to emphasise people's subjectivities and capabilities and thereby prevents processes of objectification, as Moser and Clark point out happens in many cases (2001a: 4).

Along this understanding of agency, the way women ex-combatants are dealing with the institutionally offered ideas of identities shall be analysed. Many organisations' treatment of women after the war has been found to support their victimhood and encourage them to identify as a "vulnerable group". Underneath this lies the question on how such activities are affecting women's agencies and consequently their self-images.

Being exposed to the projects mentioned above, they gain knowledge via their participation and thereby experience ways of making claims by identifying with certain categories. Participation in itself may serve to secure a livelihood for themselves and potential dependants. As such, while on the surface they are identifying as victims, underneath they make choices and are employing gainful mechanisms. This has often been portrayed as a result of the war, women being perceived as more active and assertive as a consequence of those coping mechanisms established during the conflict.

As agency is interlinked with a social actor's self-image, it can be assumed that such developments are interdependent with processes of identity construction[1]. The post-war atmosphere in Sierra Leone is perceived by some as being quite fluid, with voices asking for change and others calling for the return or maintenance of tradition and cultural norms. Turshen argues that this post-war moment may be flexible but will still not allow for any possible development of gender roles as the previously established "elite" of older men maintains a tentatively conservative control over possible developments (2001: 81)[2]. Additionally, Shaw points out that in a war, where "neighbours killed neighbours"; memory is a dangerous and highly contested issue. Public remembering is therefore discouraged by an institutionalised "social forgetting" (Shaw 2005: 3). Therefore, referring openly to wartime experiences as a foundation of post-war lives or processes of identification would mean to oppose this notion of healing society's wounds of war. Consequently, the local ideas of healing would limit women's capacity to make free use of the already contested options of identifying as ex-combatants, which are at the same time discouraged by the (re-) establishing representatives of gerontocracy, the "elite" of older men.

In this atmosphere women ex-combatants make their choices. Hypothetically these range from identifying as ex-combatants and potentially participating in the DDR programme or opting out of this and "choosing life on the street" or so-called "self-demobilisation". The other, more readily available option is associating with the fate of "bush wives" and identifying as such. While both options imply victimhood in the various programmes and public perspectives, the latter appears to be less challenging and institutionally more accessible than the former. Rather than breaking out of established gender roles they can negotiate within the recognised reference system of roles and identification, which are not destroyed but contested: "[The] conflict does not appear to have lead to a shift in gender identities, but rather to growing tensions between people's ideals (of masculinity and femininity) and the practical reality available to them" (El-Bushra 2001: 164).

While identities such as "bush wives", less than female ex-combatants would, may contribute to the post-conflict tensions, they still remain inside the established reference system. By making these choices, women consciously take upon themselves the consequences. Far from being passive victims, women ex-combatants appear to victimise themselves as a manoeuvre

1 See Moser and Clark (2001a).
2 See also Richards et al. (2003).

of protection, to thereby remain active agents of their lives. In the dire circumstances of the every-day life in rural Sierra Leone, participation in a project can mean securing a livelihood, as Mbalu and her friends Sarah and Margaret point out:

> We need this project and the income, even if it isn't much. Otherwise we have to be friends with those men[1] again. They provide for us, but that means they buy us. And we don't want to do that. But the other option is prostitution; that is even worse (*Mbalu*).

The three women prefer to identify as war victims and employ vulnerability to gain the support of the accorded status, which in turn enables them to evade other, less desirable options. Their strategising reveals knowledge of available options and the willingness to use these. With these choices, the three women are in a more advantageous position compared to women not participating in projects. To secure their and their dependants' livelihood, according to Richards et al., the latter women enter into relationships in rural environments, which resemble "domestic servitude" to "village polygynists". The authors argue that this is the result of the women having to enter "low-status marriages", not protected by male family members of a powerful lineage. They usually stay in these relationships due the shared perception of lack of alternatives. In the authors' opinion, the women not participating in projects around DDR constitute an even "more needy group" than women identifying as "bush wives" or even ex-combatants (Richards et al. 2003: 15).

Considering the above, the strategy of "self-proclaimed victimhood" that Mbalu and others employ to fit the NGO-categories of a "vulnerable group" are quite successful in preventing them from having to take up other, in their perspective less desirable roles. Rather, they use their knowledge and experience of projects to find employment or participate in new projects to secure their income (*Mbalu*). Tafere makes similar observations for Ethiopian ex-combatants who perceive themselves as a "vulnerable group" and therefore feel entitled to claim participation and benefits from NGO projects (2004: 330).

---

1 Mbalu and her friends refer to *sugar daddies*, fairy well-to-do men of a certain age providing for considerably younger longer-term "girl friends". In urban and semi-urban settings of Sierra Leone this practice is quite common.

Besides the potential roles these women take up, they seem to strategise more around projects offered than women ex-combatants who are not taking part in projects but are trying to "blend in" instead. Whether it is the programmes providing the women with this agency or whether they acquired this during the war, in the interaction they reveal a profound development of agency: identifying as victims provides the former combatants with the agency to make use of the choices offered by organisations' categorisations, which thereby turn into existing realities.

4.4 Women choosing between different realities

Observing the lack of gender mainstreaming in the Sierra Leonean DDR programme, it is clear that there was no systematically interrelated integration of women into the programme. In such circumstances it is only coherent that women faced contradictory attitudes on their varying participation in war from the side of organisations, which influenced their potential post-conflict roles. They were addressed as victims and in other parts of the programme pushed into roles of "agents of change" by being given information on women's rights and gender equality. As these ideas were not coordinated within the organisations or their programmes, women as their "target group" had to negotiate for themselves by their reactions to and interactions with the programmes offered.

Such considerations open up the hypothetical possibility that if Demobilisation had encouraged changes of gender roles to a greater extent more women would have identified as ex-combatants and later continued to strive for substantial changes of gender roles, just as Ms. Ngombeh had suggested. Following this line of thought, without outside support from civil society, the resistance within society would have been too strong to demand overt challenging of established gender roles from and by all these women. However, as there was only a limited discourse on gender roles in post-war Sierra Leone society, these contemplations appear to be redundant.

While the DDR programme was not gender mainstreamed, it still held a lot of gendered categories which, though being inconsistent, the women responded to. Women's and human rights as well as (S)GBV were topics in which messages of women's equality were conveyed and a small number of the organisations involved clearly aimed at promoting women's empowerment. By making their choices on participating in certain programmes and taking up some of their aspects, women (ex-) combatants acknowledged the fact that war has resulted in changes on their self-image and consequently on the available options of future identification.

War also takes its (direct or indirect) effects on many other social relations which in turn influence the "multiple subject positions" every person is located in within a given society (Farr 2002: 6). As a result many people face new circumstances after the war and have to negotiate their social roles and relationships anew. In this light many people wish to return to the known, the "traditional" notions of social interaction, opposing the war's chaos and instead seeking the presumed stability of the past, familiar order.

Women combatants therefore had different possibilities, determined by those gendered categories organisations made available to them. One option, identifying as an ex-combatant and participating in the designated programme became a hard one and was often an institutionally inaccessible possibility. Entering Demobilisation was associated with accepting male attributions, potentially resulting in great reprisals. In some areas this included the stigma of being labelled a rebel. Due to overlapping tasks and shared experiences, a lot of these female combatants could identify as "bush wives" along with other women who had been abducted and forced to provide services for the male fighters. In-between these two institutionalised roles was a range of other possibilities of partaking in projects under the "(S)GBV-label" promoted by some NGOs. All these programmes obliged the women to, on the surface at least, identify as victims of the war. Yet, underneath women chose within an established and available reference system and therefore found some protection and the ability to make claims in projects. Nevertheless, identifying as victims and gaining benefits on the basis of displaying their own vulnerability is a limited analysis of women's interaction with the available categories of identification.

While the possible options of post-war identifications may be limiting from an empowerment perspective, they do provide protection for those women who find themselves in the midst of competing/compromising aspects of past experiences. By identifying as a "victim of war", they can try to evade allegations of having been a combatant, a perpetrator or rebel. The labels of abducted "bush wives" or "sex slaves" are credible and may prove less harmful and at the same time more compatible to expected gender roles.

For a future perspective on long-term (re-) integration such aspects have a considerable weight. Ferme has described the strategy of gainful employment of public self-victimisation for women who wanted to end undesired marriages in the 1920's, when a divorce was hard to obtain. Once the British colonial rule abolished slavery, some women identified as "slave wives" and therefore had to be freed with the support of the colonial institutions. By embracing the "slave identity", these women managed to attain the desired divorce (Ferme 2001: 226).

While on overt acknowledgment of war resulting in changes upsetting gender relations seems impossible in the present Sierra Leonean context, women ex-combatants instead employ established reference systems of gender roles. As a consequence, on the surface gender relations might not have changed. Yet underneath, women's agencies have been enlarged and therefore enable them to negotiate the tensions that changes from the war brought about. As such, they are more able to choose between the realities of the Sierra Leone post-war situation, supported by organisations' dichotomising categories of femininities and masculinities, combatants and non-combatants, victims and perpetrators.

In this sense, DDR and related projects did take their influence and have an impact on the choices women make when coming out of the war. Even if some aim at gender equality and others are indifferent towards women's empowerment, they all convey ideas on the subject of appropriate femininities and masculinities and according behaviour.

These reflections hint to potentially missed opportunities in the post-war moment regarding the so-called "window of opportunity". This view was voiced mainly by women who belonged to the (educated) "elite" before the war and who found that, after participating in the conflict, their position had not improved substantially. From their perspective Demobilisation did not take the opportunity to establish new categories but remained within pre-war gender stereotypes. Therefore it did not challenge established gender roles of women, their rights and resulting every-day life circumstances on a broader political level as well as systematically within the public discourse. Thus, the programme failed obligations imposed by UN gender mainstreaming standards as well as other, related rights' based approaches to influence local gender politics towards the empowerment of women (*Alice*; Seifert 2004: 21).

Nevertheless, the mere presence of organisations and programmes has already impacted on the local population in a variety of ways. Many of these effects develop along gendered lines. They cover potential job opportunities like cooking for women or working as drivers for men, on the informal side they also substantially increase the level of commercial sex work and sexual violence mainly against the local female population[1]. In this light, the Namibia Plan of Action points to the need for broad-based research on the impact peacekeeping missions have on local gender dimensions, including the formal programming and its more or less conscious messages on gender relations conveyed in them. On the more informal side, implications like commercial sex work and sexual abuse of the population also need more understanding and weight attributed to them. In the Plan's terms, the impact on the "host culture" and its "development of gender relations" would benefit from greater study (UNTAG 2000 par. 8) to improve on the frequently negative impacts of military peacekeeping in general and the unintended gender dimension a mission may have in particular.

---

1 See, amongst others, Higate 2004; TRC report 2004: Vol. 3b: Chap. 3.

5 Conclusion: Challenges and changes for women's self-image

> The fact that women have been the main victims and among the leaders in the wars in this region – both historically and in the present – underscores the extent to which social practices both reproduce and transgress such cultural ideas (Ferme 2001: 62).

Even when individual lives are disrupted, challenged, upset and destroyed by warfare, conflict and war in themselves are part of most societies. Therefore (social) rules and regulations are developed and employed, enabling communities to deal with them and their consequences. Militarisation and mobilisation for a war belong to this sphere as much as strategies of appropriate warfare or the recognition of certain kinds of violence and social healing processes in its aftermath. While the post-conflict moment is perceived by some as socially more flexible, with war's upheaval taking its effects on behavioural norms and changing mainstream forms of interaction, these cannot, as Ferme points out above, be interpreted as substantial dissections of established social conventions. Rather, ideas of tradition are present and are mediating the (re-) assertion of every-day life. Due to individual experiences and observations causing people to perceive war as an upheaval and breach of "normal" life, the urge to return to pre-war conditions, implying security and stability, often finds its manifestation in the call for re-traditionalisation.

Under these conditions, women and their behaviour are given close attention due to their bodies often serving as "markers of community boundaries". As a consequence, high expectations are put on women's demeanour and are closely registered and evaluated. On the circumstance of women's behaviour challenging norms after the war, judgements are made and potentially sanctions taken as part of protecting and (re-) establishing social norms:

> Thinking ill of them [female ex-combatants] is not the way women think about those women who fought. It's the way society has made women think. And the way society has made everybody to think, not only the women (*PRIDE*).

Consequently, the situation of combatants during and after the war is not free from established roles and expectations of desirable conduct. Women ex-combatants, the main focus of this work, are facing this environment and have to decide within this context how they are going to react to the programmes brought into the country by international agencies. As such, questions of gender relations are taking place in an atmosphere influenced by more "traditional" expectations and simultaneously hopes for changes.

In this post-war moment and under the perception of challenged or more fluid social circumstances, some analysts and organisations aim to intervene in order to support those supposedly challenging or even changing tendencies and ideas. This, according to some authors, has to happen before the immediate and therefore more flexible post-war moment passes and "traditional" believes are again manifested. In the terminology of the aid industry the "social development" of a post-conflict society should be influenced with the aim to mould it according to ideas of international (legal) standard. These interventions are designed with the call to establish women's empowerment and/or equal rights.

With political goals and the intention to influence the local "development", these organisations appear to build on assumptions regarding the extent of the challenges war brought into society, which do not adhere to a socially embedded notion of war but interpret it as a rupture of social life. Only in this understanding they can claim and expect substantial changes in gender roles occurring as effects of war.

In this understanding, UN organisations are trying to employ gender mainstreaming in their interventions into conflict and post-conflict settings. While obliged to include gender into their agendas and programming due to international conventions and organisational gender action plans, the implementation has been found to be more challenging than expected (Farr 2003a: 30). Besides the question of knowledge and capabilities, the political will to implement the original ideas of gender mainstreaming can also be doubted: "The problem with international organisations and these legal agreements is that they quickly become only words and there is no monitoring or enforcement" (workshop participant, cited in Mazurana 2004: 74).

Regarding Demobilisation as one aspect of UN's post-conflict interventions, the programme in Sierra Leone can be located in this wider web of gender mainstreaming challenges within the UN. While the programme was understood as "gender neutral", it clearly included male-associated categories of target groups and according eligibility criteria. Therefore, it gave women less chances to enter unless they adhered to these notions and associated with the role of male, weapon-bearing fighters. When projects or parts of them were designed to address women's "needs", they were included into programming due to the perceived support and protection they were presumed to require. Gender mainstreaming became reduced to the integration of a "vulnerable group", with this concept holding certain implications of passive victimhood and displaying vulnerability. Therefore, instead of breaking out of essentialised femininities and masculinities by employing gendered policies, institutions conceptually remained within earlier understandings of "add women and stir" (Wharton 2005: 4). Due to the possibility of reducing transformative concepts to older understandings, it is obvious that gender mainstreaming as a tool cannot be an all-encompassing and -enabling instrument to secure equal and equitable positions of women and men within the established mechanisms of the international community.

Thus, putting the blame of "leaving behind the women" only on Demobilisation mechanisms is a restricting perspective as these are merely part of the broader conceptual and financial network of international policies and politics. DDR cannot be the all-encompassing solution for post-conflict countries, including de-militarisation, integration of combatants and development of a country. Meek and Malan depict this point very clearly, noting that purpose and scope of such programmes need to be clear and known to all participants in order to avoid manifold allegations as happened in Sierra Leone. All institutions and especially the so-called "target group" would have to be adequately informed so that no unrealistic and unrealistic expectations could be raised (Meek and Malan 2004: 52).

These considerations should not serve as an excuse for the impact DDR and related projects have on women combatants due to lack of gender mainstreaming leading to inconsistencies in gendered implications of the programme and victimisation of women.

As a consequence of these conceptual and institutional limitations, the women participating in Demobilisation would later receive inconsistent and contradictory information and treatment based on gender stereotypes of women during and after the war. These ranged from the expected male association in the disarmament process, rights' based equality as part of the information given during demobilisation to victimisation regarding their entry into the war or child-like treatment in later reintegration projects. In DDR-related programmes on (S)GBV women were addressed as victims of the conflict and gained entitlements on this basis. All these programmes certain employed assumptions on roles and their potential war-related changes based on specific ideas of masculinities and femininities. Far from being "gender neutral", Demobilisation itself and related programmes contained and took their influences on accessible categories and on options women could choose from.

Along this understanding it becomes obvious that women were not totally excluded from the DDR in Sierra Leone but given certain roles and possibilities not matching the expectations of gender mainstreaming policies within the UN system. While it is obvious that women were not given equal and equitable chances to enter and gain benefits, the continuous proclamation of women's marginalisation within the UN system only maintains or maybe even supports the perceived victimisation of women within the system.

It is upon these institutional conditions that women combatants emerged from the war and made choices on whether and how to participate in programmes. Certainly the categories offered by the organisations influence and limit these choices, but only with women engaging with them and employing them for their comparative benefit are these categories endowed with realities. By making choices and identifying with eligibility criteria, women are affected by the implied images, many times leading to inadvertent public self-victimisation in order to gain benefits and securing livelihood. In this notion no new gender roles were substantially supported in the programmes. Instead, with the "bush wife complex", established systems of reference were employed, forming recognisable boundaries of women's roles and responsibilities during the past war, offering explanations and protection. From the outside, these may be interpreted as re-traditionalising notions. As such, many organisations did not empower women in an equal-rights' sense but certainly had influence on their processes of identification.

While during the war some gender roles and relations may have been employed more flexibly due to necessity of securing survival, they still followed asserted social expectations. For example the ascription of service tasks or the expectations of submissive behaviour on the part of women within the fighting units follow established gender stereotypes. While individual women did take up certain responsibilities and tasks, a general questioning of gender relations within the wider society as the effect of the war did not take place. Even though their self-image was certainly changed due to being exposed to new circumstances calling for the establishment of coping strategies or gaining new knowledge, McKay and Mazurana point out that "coping mechanisms and resilience demonstrated" by the women during the conflict should not be mistaken as empowerment itself (2004: 120). These coping strategies and new experiences are not mirrored in a broader discourse of women's challenged gender roles but are instead often disregarded or even decried.

In this light, perceiving the war as empowering women in a rights-based understanding seems inappropriate. With broadening capabilities and extending experience, individual women certainly gained agency, which they could later employ when facing post-conflict programmes. Within many, for example the projects on (S)GBV and to a limited extent also DDR, women could capitalise on this agency and use projects to their benefit, securing livelihood and benefits. Such broadened agencies certainly also take their effects on the women's self-images and impact on their behaviour.

Accordingly, NGO-supported public identification as a "bush wife" may secure and provide a basis for these agencies to build on self-images and adjust identities. On the opposite side, as Richards et al. (2003) observed with women who did not take part in projects around DDR, denying war-related challenges and events, lived in even more dire circumstances. Being victimised and abused, these women may lack necessary agencies to change their situation and make alternative choices, potentially leading to different realities:

> Depending on the circumstances, the legacy [of the war] could either offer additional opportunities to find freedom from the constraints of binding allegiances or reproduce the potential for mutual exploitation through the denial of the same history (Ferme 2001: 226).

Therefore, while gender mainstreaming might have failed and lead projects to contain categories either not integrating women at all and instead addressing them in male-associated roles, or incorporating them as victims, some women combatants made use of these options. Employing the agency maybe gained during war, they engage with the categories put forward by the organisations and bestow them with new meaning. In doing so, women ex-combatants use the multiple interrelationships of current and past roles to transcend the dichotomised notions of victim and perpetrator, victimisation and agency, NGO categories of gender mainstreaming and their self-images.

6 Bibliography

Abdela, Lesley 2004: "Kosovo: Missed Opportunities, Lessons for the Future" in: Haleh Afshar and Deborah Eade (eds.): *Development, Women and War. Feminist Perspectives.* Oxford: Oxfam GB.

Abdullah, Ibrahim 1997: Bush Paths to Destruction: The Origin and Character of the Revolutionary United Front (RUF/SL). *Africa Development* 22/3–4: 45–76.

Afshar, Haleh and Deborah Eade (eds.) 2004: *Development, Women and War: Feminist Perspectives.* Oxford: Oxfam GB.

Alden, Chris 2002: Making old Soldiers Fade Away: Lessons from the Reintegration of Demobilised Soldiers in Mozambique. *Security Dialogue* 33/3: 341–356.

Alice, Lynne Christine 2004: "Bridging the Gender Gap: Political Culture in Kosovo" in: Ruth Seifert (ed.): *Gender, Identität und kriegerischer Konflikt. Das Beispiel des ehemaligen Jugoslawien.* Münster: Lit-Verlag.

Alie, Joe 2005: "The Kamajor Militia in Sierra Leone: Liberators or Nihilists?" in: David J. Francis (ed.): *Civil Militia: Africa's Intractable Security Menace?* Hants: Ashgate.

Aning, Emmanuel Kwesi 1998: Gender and Civil War: The Cases of Liberia and Sierra Leone. *Civil Wars* 1/4: 1–26.

Bangura, Yusuf 1997: Understanding the Political and Cultural Dynamics of the Sierra Leone War. A Critique of Paul Richards' Fighting for the Rain Forest. *Africa Development* 22/3–4: 117–148.

Barth, Elise Fredrikke 2002: *Peace as Disappointment: The Reintegration of Female Soldiers in Post-Conflict Societies: A Comparative Study from Africa.* International Peace Research Institute Oslo. <www.peacewomen.org/resoureces/DDR/AfricaBarth.html> [3rd October 2004].

Beilstein, Janet 1998: "The Expanding Role of Women in United Nations Peacekeeping" in: Lois Ann Lorentzen and Jennifer Turpin (eds.): *The Women and War Reader.* New York: New York University Press.

Bennett, Olivia, Jo Bexley and Kitty Warnock 1995: *Arms to Fights, Arms to Protect: Women Speak out about Conflict.* London: Panos.
Bereswill, Mechtild 2005: Im toten Winkel. Zwiespältiges Bild: Gender Mainstreaming macht Geschlecht zur bloßen Humanressource. *Freitag* 43 (28.10.2005).
< www.freitag.de/2005/43/ 05431701.php> [03.11.2005].
Bilgin, Pinar 2004: International Politics of Women's (In)security: Rejoinder to Mary Caprioli. *Security Dialogue* 35/4: 499–504.
Bop, Codou 2001: "Women in Conflict, Their Gains and Their Losses" in: Sheila Meintjes, Anu Pillay and Meredeth Turshen (eds.): *The Aftermath: Women in Post-Conflict Transformation.* London: Zed Books.
Bourdieu, Pierre 2001: *Masculine Domination.* Cambridge: Polity Press.
Bouta, Tsjeard, Georg Frerks and Ian Bannon 2005: *Gender, Conflict, and Development.* Washington: The International Bank for Reconstruction and Development/The World Bank.
Bracken, Patrick J. 1998: "Hidden Agendas: Deconstructing Post Traumatic Stress Disorder" in: Patrick J. Bracken and Celia Petty (eds.): *Rethinking the Trauma of War.* London: Free Association Books ltd.
Byman, Daniel L. 2001: Uncertain Partners: NGOs and the Military. *Survival* 43/2: 97–114.
Campbell, Greg 2002: *Blood Diamonds: Tracing the Deadly Path of the World's Most Precious Stones.* Boulder: Westview Press.
Caplan, Pat 1992: "Engendering Knowledge: The Politics of Ethnography" in: Shirley Ardener (ed.): *Persons and Powers of Women in Diverse Cultures.* New York: Berg.
Caprioli, Mary 2000: Gendered Conflict. *Journal of Peace Research* 37/1: 51–68.
Caprioli, Mary 2004: Democracy and Human Rights versus Women's Security: A Contradiction?. *Security Dialogue* 35/4: 411–428.
Caprioli, Mary and Mark A. Boyer 2001: Gender, Violence and International Crisis. *The Journal of Conflict Resolution* 45/4: 503–518.
Cartwright, John R. 1970: *Politics in Sierra Leone 1947–67.* Toronto: University of Toronto Press.
Cassell, Catherine and Sue Walsh 1997: Organizational Psychology: Research/Practice Organisational Cultures, Gender Management Strategies and Women's Experience of Work. *Feminism and Psychology: An International Journal* 7/2: 224–230.

Cimet, Adina 2002: “Symbolic Violence and Language: Mexico and its Use of Symbols“ in: Jacob. J. Climo and Maria G. Cattell (eds.): *Social Memory and History: Anthropological Perspectives.* Walnut Creek: AltaMira Press.

Christophe, Barbara 2004: “Inszenierung von Scheinkonflikten als Strategie. Die Unsichtbarkeit der Macht in Georgien” in: Julia M. Eckert (ed.): *Anthropologie der Konflikte. Georg Elwerts konflikttheoretische Thesen in der Diskussion.* Bielfeld: transcript Verlag.

Colletta, Nat, Markus Kostner and Ingo Wiederhofer 1996: *The Transition from War to Peace in Sub-Saharan Africa.* Washington: The World Bank.

Collier, Jane F. 1997: *From Duty to Desire: Remaking Families in a Spanish Village.* Princeton: Princeton University Press.

Conthe-Morgan, Earl and Mac Dixon-Fyle 1999: *Sierra Leone at the End of the Twentieth Century. History, Politics and Society.* New York: Peter Lang.

Cockburn, Cynthia 2001: “The Gendered Dynamics of Armed Conflict and Political Violence” in: Caroline O.N. Moser and Fiona C. Clark (eds.): *Victims, Perpetrators or Actors? Gender, Armed Conflict and Political Violence.* London: Zed Books.

Cordero, Isabel Coral 2001: “Social Organisations: From Victims to Actors in Peace Building” in: Caroline O.N. Moser and Fiona C. Clark (eds.): *Victims, Perpetrators or Actors? Gender, Armed Conflict and Political Violence.* London: Zed Books.

Corrin, Chris 2004: “Geschlechterverhältnisse und Friedensprozesse: Gender in der Nachkriegs-Rekonstruktion in Kosova” in: Ruth Seifert (ed.): *Gender, Identität und kriegerischer Konflikt. Das Beispiel des ehemaligen Jugoslawien.* Münster: Lit-Verlag.

Coulter, Chris 2005: Reflections from the Field: A Girl’s Initiation Ceremony in Northern Sierra Leone. *African Quarterly* 78/2: 431–441.

D’Amico, Francine 1998: “Feminist Perspectives on Women Warriors” in Lois Ann Lorentzen and Jennifer Turpin (eds.): *The Women and War Reader.* New York: New York University Press.

Debiel, Tobias 2002: *UN-Friedenssicherung in Subsahara-Afrika: Möglichkeiten und Grenzen mulitlateraler Konfliktbearbeitung in regionalisierten Bürgerkriegen; eine Untersuchung im Rahmen des Global-Governance-Ansatzes.* Duisburg: Institut für Entwicklung und Frieden.

DeKeseredy, Walter S. and Martin D. Schwartz 2005: "Masculinities and Interpersonal Violence" in: Michael S. Kimmel, Jeff Hearn and Robert W. Connell (eds.): *Men and Masculinities.* Thousand Oaks: Sage Publications.

Deng, Francis M. 1998: *Internally Displaced Persons: Compilation and Analysis of Legal Norms.* New York: United Nations. (Human Rights Study Series No.9).

Dixon-Fyle, Mac and Gibril Cole (eds.) 2006: *New Perspectives on the Sierra Leone Krio.* New York: Peter Lang.

Du Nann Winter, Deborah, Marc Pilisuk, Sara Houck and Matthew Lee 2001: "Understanding Militarism: Money, Masculinity and the Search for the Mystical" in: Daniel J. Christie, Richard V. Wagner and Deborah Du Nann Winter (eds.): *Peace, Conflict and Violence. Peace Psychology for the 21st Century.* Upper Saddle River: Prentice Hall.

Eade, Deborah 2004: "Preface" in: Haleh Afshar and Deborah Eade (eds.): *Development, Women and War – Feminist Perspectives.* Oxford: Oxfam GB.

Eifler, Christine 2000: Militär, Gender und "Peacekeeping" – zu einem widersprüchlichen Verhältnis. *femina politica* 9/1: 37–47.

Eifler, Christine 2004: "Genderkompetenz und militärisches Handeln in Krisengebieten und Nachkriegsgesellschaften – eine Problemskizze" in: Ruth Seifert (ed.): *Gender, Identität und kriegerischer Konflikt. Das Beispiel des ehemaligen Jugoslawien.* Münster: Lit-Verlag.

El-Bushra, Judy 2004: "Fused in Combat: Gender Relations and Armed Conflict" in: Haleh Afshar and Deborah Eade (eds.): *Development, Women and War – Feminist Perspectives.* Oxford: Oxfam GB.

Elwert, Georg 1999: "Markets of Violence" in: Georg Elwert, Stephan Feuchtwang and Dieter Neubert (eds.): *Dynamics of Violence. Processes of Escalation and De-Escalation in Violent Group Conflicts.* Berlin: Duncker & Humblot.

Elwert, Georg 2004: "Anthropologische Perspektiven auf Konflikte" in: Julia M. Eckert (ed.): *Anthropologie der Konflikte. Georg Elwerts konflikttheoretische Thesen in der Diskussion.* Bielefeld: transcript Verlag.

Enloe, Cynthia 2000: *Maneuvers – The international Politics of Militarising Women's Lives.* Berkeley: University of California Press.

Farr, Vanessa 2002: *Gendering Demobilisation as a Peacekeeping Tool.* Bonn: Bonn International Centre for Conversion. (BICC paper 20).

Farr, Vanessa 2003a: Women, Men and the Struggle to Disarm. *Conflict Trends* 3: 26–31.

Farr, Vanessa 2003b: The Importance of a Gender Perspective to Successful Disarmament, Demobilisation and Reintegration Processes. *disarmament forum* 4: 25–35.

Feldman, Allen 1995: "Ethnographic States of Emergency" in: Carolyn Nordstrom and Antonius C.G.M. Robben (eds.): *Fieldwork under Fire: Contemporary Studies of Violence and Survival.* Berkeley: University of California Press.

femina politica 2004: Essentialisierung durch Gender Mainstreaming? Dialog mit Annemarie Sancar über die geschlechterpolitischen Folgen eines Politikinstruments am Beispiel des Wassersektors. *femina politica* 2: 15–38.

Ferguson, Richard Brian 1990: "Explaining War" in: J. Haas (ed.): *The Anthropology of War.* Cambridge: Cambridge University Press.

Ferme, Mariane C. 2001: *The Underneath of Things: Violence, History and the Everyday in Sierra Leone.* Berkeley: University of California Press.

Flood, Michael 2005: "Men's Collective Struggle for Gender Justice: The Case of Antiviolence Activism" in: Michael S. Kimmel, Jeff Hearn and Robert W. Connell (eds.): *Men and Masculinities.* Thousand Oaks: Sage Publications.

Foray, Michael 2000: "Peace by Other Means: The Missing Link in DDR Programmes" in: Anatole Ayissi and Robin-Edward Poulton (eds.): *Bound to Cooperate: Conflict, Peace and People in Sierra Leone.* Geneva: United Nations Institute for Disarmament Research.

Foucault, Michel 1978: *The History of Sexuality.* Harmondsworth: Penguin Books.

Fuest, Veronika 1999: "Modernes" Wissen – "moderne" Macht. Zur kulturellen Konstruktion formaler Bildung am Beispiel von Geheimbund-Gesellschaften in Liberia und Sierra Leone. *Zeitschrift für Ethnologie* 124/1: 73–95.

Galtung, Johan 1985: "Military Formations and Social Formations: a Structural Analysis" in: Peter Wallensteen, Johan Galtung and Carlos Portales (eds.): *Global Militarisation.* Boulder: Westview Press.

Gberie, Lansana 2004: *Diamonds without Map: Liberia, the UN, Sanctions and the Kimberley Process; Special Report.* Ottawa: Partnership Africa Canada.

Gberie, Lansana 2005: *A dirty war in West Africa. The RUF and the destruction of Sierra Leone.* London: Hurst and Company.
Gedalof, Irene 1999: *Against Purity: Rethinking Identity with Indian and Western Feminisms.* London: Routledge.
Goffman, Ervin 1961: *Asylums: Essays on the Social Situation of Mental Patients and other Inmates.* Chicago: Aldine.
Goldstein, Joshua S. 2001: *War and Gender: How Gender Shapes the War System and Vice Versa.* Cambridge: Cambridge University Press.
Green, December 1999: *Gender Violence in Africa: African Women's Responses.* London: Macmillan.
Gudmundur, Alfredsson and Katarina Tomasevski 1995: *A Thematic Guide to Documents on the Human Rights of Women*, Part 1. Cambridge: Kluwer Law International.
Hagemann-White, Carol and Hans-Joachim Lenz 2004: "Violence against Women/Violence against Men: Comparisons, Differences, Controversies" in: Renate Klein and Bernd Wallner (eds.): *Conflict, Gender and Violence.* Innsbruck: Studienverlag.
Hale, Sondra 2001: "Liberated, But Not Free: Women in Post-War Eritrea" in: Sheila Meintjes, Anu Pillay and Meredeth Turshen (eds.): *The Aftermath: Women in Post-Conflict Transformation.* London: Zed Books.
Hauser-Schäublin, Brigitta 2002: "Gender: Verkörperte Feldforschung" in: Hans Fischer (ed.): *Feldforschung – Erfahrungsberichte zur Einführung.* Berlin: Dietrich Reimer Verlag.
Hearn, Jeff 2001: Men Stopping Men's Violence to Women. *Development* 4(3): 85–89.
Heyzer, Noeleen 2003: Gender, Peace and Disarmament. *disarmament forum* 4: 6–16.
Higate, Paul 2004: "Peacekeepers and Gender: DRC and Sierra Leone". <www.peacewomen.org/un/pkwatch/News/04/Higateeditorial.html> [21st September 2004].
Higate, Paul and John Hopton 2005: "War, Militarism and Masculinities" in: Michael S. Kimmel, Jeff Hearn and Robert W. Connell (eds.): *Men and Masculinities.* Thousand Oaks: Sage Publications.
Hoffer, Carol P. 1972: Mende and Sherbro Women in High Office. *Canadian Journal of African Studies* 6/2: 151–164.

Human Rights Watch (HRW) 2003: *We'll Kill You If You cry.* New York: Human Rights Watch.

Humphreys, Macartan and Jeremy Weinstein 2004: *What the Fighters Say: A Survey of Ex-Combatants in Sierra Leone*, June–August 2003. Interim Report: July 2004. <www.columbia.edu/ ~mh2245/Report1_BW.pdf> [15th August 2004].

Humphreys, Macartan and Jeremy Weinstein 2005: *Handling and Manhandling Civilians in Civil Wars: Determinants in the Strategies of Warring Factions.* <www.columbia.edu/~mh2245/papers1/Civilians.pdf> [23rd February 2005].

Ináñez, Ana Cristina 2001: "El Salvador: War and Untold Stories. Women Guerillas" in: Caroline O.N. Moser and Fiona C. Clark (eds.): *Victims, Perpetrators or Actors? Gender, Armed Conflict and Political Violence.* London: Zed Books.

Jacobs, Susie, Ruth Jacobson and Jennifer Marchbank 2000: "Introduction: States of Conflict" in: Susie Jacobs, Ruth Jacobson and Jennifer Marchbank (eds.): States of Conflict: *Gender, Violence and Resistance.* London: Zed Books.

Kai-Kai, Francis Dr. 2000: "Disarmament, Demobilisation and Reintegration in post-war Sierra Leone" in: Anatol Ayissi and Robin Edward Poiulton (eds.): *Bound to Cooperate: Conflict, Peace and People in Sierra Leone.* Geneva: United Nations Institute for Disarmament Research.

Kandiyoti, Deniz 1991: "Introduction" in: Deniz Kandiyoti (ed.): *Women, Islam and the State.* London: Macmillan.

Kaminski, Marek M. 2003: Games Prisoners Play: Allocation of Social Roles in a Total Institution. *Rationality and Society* 15/2: 189–218.

Katayanagi, Mari 2002: *Human Rights Functions of United Nations Peacekeeping Operations.* The Hague: Nijhoff.

Keen, David 2005: *Conflict and Collusion in Sierra Leone.* New York: Palgrave.

Kegan Gardiner, Judith 2005: "Men, Masculinities and Feminist Theory" in: Michael S. Kimmel, Jeff Hearn and Robert W. Connell (eds.): *Men and Masculinities.* Thousand Oaks: Sage Publications.

Kelly, Liz 2000: "Wars Against Women: Sexual Violence, Sexual Politics and the Militarised State" in: Susie Jacobs, Ruth Jacobson and Jennifer Marchbank (eds.): *States of Conflict: Gender, Violence and Resistance.* London: Zed Books.

Kilson, Martin 1966: *Political Change in a West African State: A Study of the Modernization Process in Sierra Leone.* Cambridge: Harvard University Press.

Kimmel, Michael, Jeff Hearn and Robert Connell (eds.) 2005: *Men and Masculinities.* Thousand Oaks: Sage Publications.

Kingma, Kees (ed.) 2000: *Demobilisation in Sub-Saharan Africa. The Development and Security Impacts.* London: Macmillan Press.

Kligman, Gail 1998: *The Politics of Duplicity: Controlling Reproduction in Ceausescu's Romania.* Berkeley: University of California Press.

Knight, Mark and Alpaslan Özerdem 2004: Guns, Camps and Cash: Disarmament, Demobilisation and Reinsertation of Former Combatants in Transition from War to Peace. *Journal of Peace Research* 41/4: 499–516.

Knörr, Jacqueline 1995: *Kreolisierung versus Pidginisierung als Kategorien kultureller Differenzierung: Varianten neoafrikanischer Identität und Interethnik in Freetown/Sierra Leone.* Münster: Lit-Verlag.

Knörr, Jacqueline and Barbara Meier 2000: "Women and Migration: Anthropological Perspectives" in: Jacqueline Knörr and Barbara Meier (eds.): *Women and Migration: Anthropological Perspectives.* Frankfurt/Main: Campus Verlag.

Koopmans, Ruud and Paul Statham 2001: "How National Citizenship Shapes Transnationalism: A Comparative Analysis of Migrant Claims-Making in Germany, Great Britain and the Netherlands" forthcoming in: Christian Joppke and Ewa Moravska (eds.): *Towards Assimilation and Citizenship: Immigrants in Liberal Nation-States.* Basingstoke: Palgrave Macmillan.

Kvande, Elin and Bente Rasmussen 1995: Women's career in static and dynamic organisations. *Acta Sociologica* 38/2: 115–130.

Lamb, Guy 2000: Reflections on Demilitarisation: A Southern African Perspective. *International Peacekeeping* 7/3: 120–136.

Le Sage, Andre L. 1998: Engaging the Political Economy of Conflict: Towards a Radical Humanitarianism. *Civil Wars* 1/4: 27–55.

Leslie, Helen 2001: Healing the Psychological Wounds of Gender-Related Violence in Latin America: a Model for Gender-Sensitive Work in Post-Conflict Contexts. *Gender and Development* 9/3: 50–59.

Lorentzen, Lois Ann and Jennifer Turpin (eds.) 1998: *The Women and War Reader.* New York: New York University Press.

Macdonald, Sharon 1987: "Drawing the Lines – Gender, Peace and War: an Introduction" in: Sharon Macdonald, Pat Holden and Shirley Ardener (eds.): *Images of women in war and peace. Cross-Cultural and Historical Perspectives.* London: Macmillan.

Mackay, Angela 2004: "Training the Uniforms: Gender and Peacekeeping Operations" in: Haleh Afshar and Deborah Eade (eds.): *Development, Women and War – Feminist Perspectives.* Oxford: Oxfam GB.

Mallan, Mark, Phenyo Rakate and Angela McIntyre 2002: *Peacekeeping in Sierra Leone: UNAMSIL hits the Home Straight.* Pretoria: Institute for Security Studies. (Monograph No. 68).

Manchanda, Rita 2001: "Ambivalent Gains in South Asian Conflicts" in: Sheila Meintjes, Anu Pillay and Meredeth Turshen (eds.): *The Aftermath: Women in Post-Conflict Transformation.* London: Zed Books.

Mansaray, Binta 2000: "Women against Weapons: a Leading Role for Women in Disarmament" in: Anatole Ayissi and Robin-Edward Poulton (eds.): *Bound to Cooperate: Conflict, Peace and People in Sierra Leone.* Geneva: United Nations Institute for Disarmament Research.

Marcaillou, Agnès 2003: The Gender Action Plan for the UN Department for Disarmament Affairs. *disarmament forum* 4: 47–52.

Mazurana, Dyan 2004: *Women in Armed Opposition Groups speak on War, Protection and Obligations under International Humanitarian and Human Rights Law.* Workshop Report for Geneva Call and the Programme for the Study of International Organisation(s). <www.genevacall.org/news/testi-events/gc-29aug04-long.pdf> [23rd January 2005].

Mazurana, Dyan and Khristopher Carlson 2004: *From Combat to Community: Women and Girls in Sierra Leone.* <www.womenwagingpeace.net/content/articles/SierraLeoneFullCase Study.pdf > [14th May 2004].

Mazurana, Dyan, Susan McKay, Khristopher Carlson and Janel Kasper 2002: "Girls in Fighting Forces and Groups: Their Recruitment, Participation, Demobilisation and Reintegration" in: *Peace and Conflict: Journal of Peace Psychology* 8/2: 97–123.

Mazurana, Dyan, Angela Raven-Roberts and Jane Parpart (eds.) 2005a: *Gender, Conflict and Peacekeeping*. Lanham: Rowman & Littlefield Publishers.

Mazurana, Dyan, Angela Raven-Roberts, Jane Parpart and Sue Lautze 2005b: "Introduction: Gender, Conflict and Peacekeeping" in: Dyan Mazurana, Angela Raven-Roberts and Jane Parpart (eds.): *Gender, Conflict and Peacekeeping*. Lanham: Rowman & Littlefield Publlishers.

McKay, Susan and Dyan Mazurana 2004: *Where are the Girls? Girls in Fighting Forces in Northern Uganda, Sierra Leone and Mozambique: Their Lives During and After War*. Montréal: International Centre for Human Rights and Democratic Development.

Meek, Sarah and Mark Malan (eds.) 2004: *Identifying Lessons from DDR Experiences in Africa*. Pretoria: Institute for Security Studies. (Monograph No. 106).

Meintjes, Sheila 2001: "War and Post-War Shifts in Gender Relations" in: Sheila Meintjes, Anu Pillay and Meredeth Turshen (eds.): *The Aftermath: Women in Post-Conflict Transformation*. London: Zed Books.

Meintjes, Sheila, Anu Pillay and Meredeth Turshen 2001: "There Is No Aftermath for Women" in: Sheila Meintjes, Anu Pillay and Meredeth Turshen (eds.): *The Aftermath: Women in Post-Conflict Transformation*. London: Zed Books.

Merry, Sally E. 2005: "Human Rights and Global Legal Pluralism: Reciprocity and Disjuncture" in: Franz von Benda-Beckmann, Keebet von Benda-Beckmann and Anne Griffiths (eds.): *Mobile People. Mobile Law: Expanding Legal Relations in a Contradicting World*. Hants: Ashgate.

Miller, Derek, Daniel Ladouceur and Zoe Dugal 2006: *From Research to Road Map: Learning from the Arms for Development Initiative in Sierra Leone*. Geneva: United nations Institute for Disarmament Research.

Molloy, Desmond 2004: The Gender Perspective as a Deterrent to Spoilers: The Sierra Leone experience. *Conflict Trends* 2: 16–19.

Molyneux, Maxine 1985: Mobilization Without Emancipation? Women's Interests, the State, and Revolution in Nicaragua. *Feminist Studies* 11/2: 227–254.

Moser, Caroline O.N. 2001: "The Gendered Continuum of Violence and Conflict: An Operational Framework" in: Caroline O.N. Moser and Fiona C. Clark (eds.): *Victims, Perpetrators or Actors? Gender, Armed Conflict and Political Violence.* London: Zed Books.

Moser, Caroline O.N. and Fiona C. Clark 2001a: "Introduction" in: Caroline O.N. Moser and Fiona C. Clark (eds.): *Victims, Perpetrators or Actors? Gender, Armed Conflict and Political Violence.* London: Zed Books.

Moser, Caroline O.N. and Fiona C. Clark 2001b: Gender, Conflict and Building Sustainable Peace: Recent Lessons from Latin America. *Gender and Development* 9/3: 29–39.

Morrell, Robert (ed.) 2001: *Changing Men in Southern Africa.* London: Zed Books.

Muana, Patrick K. 1997: The Kamajoi Militia: Civil War, Internal Displacement and the Politics of Counter-Insurgency. *Africa Development* 22/3–4: 77–100.

Myrttinen, Henri 2003: Disarming Masculinities. *disarmament forum* 4: 37–46.

Nagel, Joane 1999: "Ethnic Troubles: Gender, Sexuality and the Construction of National Identity" in: Hanspeter Kriesi, Klaus Armingeon, Hannes Siegrist and Andreas Wimmer (eds.): *Nation and National Identity: The European Expereince in Perspective.* Chur: Rüegger.

Nagel, Joane 2003: *Race, Ethnicity and Sexuality: Intimate Intersections, Forbidden Frontiers.* New York: Oxford University Press.

Nagel, Joane 2005: "Nation" in: Michael S. Kimmel, Jeff Hearn and Robert W. Connell (eds.): *Men and Masculinities.* Thousand Oaks: Sage Publications.

Nordstrom, Carolyn 1995: "War on the Front Lines" in: Carolyn Nordstrom and Antonius C.G.M. Robben (eds.): *Fieldwork under Fire: Contemporary Studies of Violence and Survival.* Berkeley: University of California Press.

Nordstrom, Carolyn 1996: Girls behind the (Front)Lines. *Peace Review* 8/3: 403–409.

Nordstrom, Carolyn 2001: "Out of the shadows" in: Thomas M. Callaghy, Ronald Kassimir and Robert Latham (eds.): *Intervention and Transnationalism in Africa: Global-Local Networks of Power.* Cambridge: Cambridge University Press.

Okome, Mojúbàlolú Olúfúnké 2001: *African Women and Power: Reflections on the perils of unwarranted Cosmopolitanism.* Jenda: A Journal of Culture and African Women Studies 1/1:1–15. <www.jendajournal.com/jenda/vol1.1/okome-.html> [14th May 2003].

Olsson, Louise 1999: *Gendering UN Peacekeeping. Mainstreaming a Gender Perspective in Multidimensional Peacekeeping Operations.* Uppsala: Uppsala University. (Department of Peace and Conflict Research Report No.53).

Olsson, Louise 2005: "The Namibia Peace Operation in a Gender Context" in: Dyan Mazurana, Angela Raven-Roberts and Jane Parpart (eds.): *Gender, Conflict and Peacekeeping.* Lanham: Rowman & Littlefield Publishers.

Orywal, Erwin 1996: "Krieg und Frieden in den Wissenschaften" in: Orywal, Erwin, Aparna Rao and Michael Bollig (eds.): *Krieg und Kampf. Die Gewalt in unseren Köpfen.* Berlin: Dietrich Reimer Verlag.

Orywal, Erwin, Aparna Rao and Michael Bollig (eds.) 1996: *Krieg und Kampf. Die Gewalt in unseren Köpfen.* Berlin: Dietrich Reimer Verlag.

Osman, Mohamed Awad 2003: *The United Nations and Peace Enforcement: Wars, Terrorism and Democracy.* Aldershot: Ashgate.

Oyewumi, Oyeronke 2001: Ties that (Un)Bind: Feminism, Sisterhood and other Foreign Relations. *Jenda: A Journal of Culture and African Women Studies* 1/1: 1–18. <www. jendajournal.com/vol1.1/oyewumi.html > [14th May 2003].

Oyewumi, Oyeronke 2002: Conceptualising Gender: The Euro-centric Foundations of Feminists Conceptions and the Challenge of African Epistemologies. *Jenda: A Journal of Culture and African Women Studies* 2/1: 1–9. <www.jendajournal.com/vol2.1/oyewumi.html> [14th May 2003].

Pankhurst, Donna 2004: "The 'Sex War' and Other Wars: Towards a Feminist Approach to Peace Building" in: Haleh Afshar and Deborah Eade (eds.): *Development, Women and War – Feminist Perspectives.* Oxford: Oxfam GB.

Pease, Bob 2000: *Recreating Men: Postmodern Masculinity Politics.* London: Sage.
Peters, Krijn and Paul Richards 1998: "Fighting With Open Eyes: Youth Combatants Talking About War in Sierra Leone" in: Patrick J. Bracken and Celia Petty (eds.): *Rethinking the Trauma of War.* London: Free Association Books Ltd.
Physicians for Human Rights (PHR) 2002: *War-Related Sexual Violence in Sierra Leone.* Boston: Physicians for Human Rights.
Puechguirbal, Nadine 2003a: Women and Peacekeeping in the Democratic Republic of Congo: Towards a Common Goal. *Conflict Trends* 3: 23–25.
Puechguirbal, Nadine 2003b: Gender Training for Peacekeepers: Lessons from the DRC. *International Peacekeeping* 10/4: 113–128.
Raven-Roberts, Angela 2005: "Gender Mainstreaming in United Nation Peacekeeping Operations: Talking the Talk, Tripping over the Walk" in: Dyan Mazurana, Angela Raven-Roberts and Jane Parpart (eds.): *Gender, Conflict and Peacekeeping.* Lanham: Rowman & Littlefield Publishers.
Reimann, Cordula 2000: *Konfliktbearbeitung in Theorie und Praxis: Spielt "Gender" eine Rolle?* Bonn: AFB Texte.
Reno, William 2001: "How Sovereignty Matters: International Markets and the Political Economy of Local Politics in Weak States" in: Thomas M. Callaghy, Ronald Kassimir and Robert Latham (eds.): *Intervention and Transnationalism in Africa: Global-Local Networks of Power.* Cambridge: Cambridge University Press.
Richards, Paul 1996: *Fighting for the Rain Forest: War; Youth and Resources in Sierra Leone.* Oxford: James Currey.
Richards, Paul 2002: Militia Conscription in Sierra Leone: Recruitment of Young Fighters in an African War. *The Comparative Study of Conscription into the Armed Forces* 20: 255–276.
Richards, Paul and Steven Archibald 2002: Seeds and Rights: New Approaches to Post-War Rehabilitation in Sierra Leone. *Disaster* 26/4: 356–367.
Richards, Paul, Steven Archibald, Khadija Bah and James Vincent 2003: *Where have all the Young People gone? Transitioning Ex-Combatants Towards Community Reconstruction after the War in Sierra Leone.* (Unpublished manuscript).

Richards, Paul, Khadija Bah and James Vincent 2004: *Social Capital and Survival: Prospects for Community-Driven Development in Post-Conflict Sierra Leone.* Washington: World Bank. (Social Development Papers No.12.).

Richmond, Oliver P. 2003: Introduction: NGOs, Peace and Humanitarian Security. *International Peacekeeping* 10/1: 1–11.

Richter-Lyonette, Elenor 2004: "Gender: Beobachtungen einer Praktikerin internationaler Zusammenarbeit" in: Ruth Seifert (ed.): *Gender, Identität und kriegerischer Konflikt. Das Beispiel des ehemaligen Jugoslawien.* Münster: Lit-Verlag.

Robben, Antonius C.G.M. and Carolyn Nordstrom 1995: "The Anthropology and Ethnography of Violence and Socio-Political Conflict" in: Carolyn Nordstrom and Antonius C.G.M. Robben (eds.): *Fieldwork under Fire: Contemporary Studies of Violence and Survival.* Berkeley: University of California Press.

Rothschild, Joyce and Cecilia Davies 1994: Organisations through the Lens of Gender: Introduction to the Special Issue. *Human Relations* 47/6: 583–590.

Salih, Sara 2002: *Judith Butler*. London: Routledge.

Sawyer, Amos 2004: Violent Conflicts and Governance Challenges in West Africa: the Case of the Mano River Basin Area. *Journal of Modern African Studies* 42/3: 437–463.

Schäfer, Rita 1990: *Die Sande-Frauengeheimgesellschaft der Mende in Sierra Leone: ihre Organisation und Masken im zeitlichen, intra- und interethnischen Vergleich.* Bonn: Holos Verlag.

Schäfer, Rita 1995: *Frauenorganisationen und Entwicklungszusammenarbeit. Traditionelle und moderne afrikanische Frauenzusammenschlüsse im interethnischen Vergleich.* Pfaffenweiler: Centaurus-Verlagsgesellschaft.

Scheper-Hughes, Nancy and Philippe Bourgois (eds.) 2004: *Violence in War and Peace: an Anthology.* Malden: Blackwell.

Schlehe, Judith 2003: "Formen qualitativer ethnographischer Interviews" in: Bettine Beer (ed.): *Methoden und Techniken der Feldforschung.* Berlin: Reimer.

Seifert, Ruth (ed.) 2004: *Gender, Identität und kriegerischer Konflikt. Das Beispiel des ehemaligen Jugoslawien.* Münster: Lit-Verlag.

Shaw, Rosalind 1992: “Dreaming as Accomplishment: Power, the Individual and the Temne Divination” in: M.C. Jędrej and Rosalind Shaw (eds.): *Dreaming, Religion and Society in Africa.* Leiden: E.J. Brill.

Shaw, Rosalind 2002: *Memories of the Slave Trade: Ritual and the Historic Imagination in Sierra Leone.* Chicago: University of Chicago Press.

Shaw, Rosalind 2005: *Rethinking Truth and Reconciliation Commissions: Lessons from Sierra Leone.* United States Institute of Peace. (Special Report 130).
<www.usip.org/pubs/specialreports/sr130.pdf> [17th May 2005].

Sideris, Tina 2001: “Problems of Identity, Solidarity and Reconciliation” in: Sheila Meintjes, Anu Pillay and Meredeth Turshen (eds.): *The Aftermath: Women in Post-Conflict Transformation.* London: Zed Books.

Skjelsbaek, Inger 1997: *Gendered Battlefields: A Gendered Analysis of Peace and Conflict.* Oslo: International Peace Research Institute. (PRIO Report No.6).

Skjelsbaek, Inger 2001: “Is Femininity Inherently Peaceful? The Construction of Femininity in War” in: Inger Skjelsbaek and Dan Smith (eds.): *Gender, Peace and Conflict.* London: Sage.

Skjelsbaek, Inger and Dan Smith 2001: “Introduction” in: Inger Skjelsbaek and Dan Smith (eds.): *Gender, Peace and Conflict.* London: Sage.

Stiehm, Judith Hicks 1997: Peacekeeping and Peace Research: Men’s and Women’s Work. *Women & Politics* 18/1: 27–51.

Tafere, Yisak 2004: “Socio-Economic Reintegration of Ex-Soldiers. A Case of two Cooperatives in Addis Ababa” in: Alula Pankhurst and François Piguet (eds.): *People, Space and the State. Migration, Resettlement and Displacement in Ethiopia.* Addis Ababa: Ethiopian Society of Sociologists, Social Workers and Anthropologists.

Thompson, Martha and Deborah Eade 2004: “Women and War: Protection through Empowerment in El Salvador” in: Haleh Afshar and Deborah Eade (eds.): *Development, Women and War – Feminist Perspectives.* Oxford: Oxfam GB.

Tickner, J. Ann 1999: Why Women Can’t Run the World: International Politics according to Francis Fukuyama. *International Studies Quarterly* 43/3: 3–11.

Turpin, Jennifer 1998: “Many Faces: Women Confronting War” in: Lois Ann Lorentzen and Jennifer Turpin (eds.): *The Women and War Reader.* New York: New York University Press.

Turshen, Meredeth 2001: “Engendering Relations of State to Society in the Aftermath” in: Sheila Meintjes, Anu Pillay and Meredeth Turshen (eds.): *The Aftermath: Women in Post-Conflict Transformation.* London: Zed Books.

Turshen, Meredeth and Clothilde Twagiramariya (eds.) 1998: *What Women Do in Wartime. Gender and Conflict in Africa.* London: Zed Books.

Utas, Mats 2005a: Victimcy, Girlfriending, Soldiering: Tracing Agency in a Young Women’s Social Navigation of the Liberian War Zone. *African Quarterly* 78/2: 403–430.

Utas, Mats 2005b: “Agency of Victims: Young Women in the Liberian Civil War” in: Alcinda Honwana and Filip De Boeck (eds.): *Makers and Breakers: Children and Youth in Postcolonial Africa.* Oxford: James Currey.

Väyrynen, Tarja 2004: Gender and UN Peace Operations: The Confines of Modernity. *International Peacekeeping* 11/1: 125–142.

Vincent, Louise Dr. 2003: Current Discourse on the Role of Women in Conflict Prevention and Conflict Transformation: a Critique. *Conflict Trends* 3: 5–10.

Volman, Daniel 1998: “The Militarization of Africa” in: Meredeth Turshen and Clothilde Twagiramariya (eds.): *What Women Do in Wartime. Gender and Conflict in Africa.* London: Zed Books.

Watteville, Natalie de 2002: *Addressing Gender Issues in Demobilisation and Reintegration Programmes.* Washington: The World Bank. (Africa Region Working Paper Series).

Weinstein, Jeremy and Macartan Humphreys 2005: *Disentangling the Determinants of Successful Demobilization and Reintegration.* Center for Global Development Working Paper No. 69. <www.cgdev.org/content/publications/detail/4155> [5th December 2005].

Werbner, Pnina and Nira Yuval-Davis 1999: “Introduction” in: Nira Yuval-Davis and Pnina Werbner (eds.): *Women, Citizenship and Difference.* London: Zed Books.

Wharton, Amy S. 2005: *The Sociology of Gender. An Introduction to Theory and Research.* Oxford: Blackwell.

White, E. Frances 1987: *Sierra Leone’s Settler Women Traders. Women on the Afro-European Frontier.* Ann Arbor: University of Michigan Press.

Wichterich, Christa 2005: From Margin to Mainstream to Margin: Wege und Umwege transnationaler Frauennetzwerke und der Globalisierung von Frauenrechten. *Peripherie* 100/25: 534–538.

Wright, Clive 2004: Tackling Conflict Diamonds: the Kimberley Process Certification Scheme. *International Peacekeeping* 11/4: 697–708.

Wyse, Akintola 1989: *The Krio of Sierra Leone: An Interpretative History.* London: Hurst & Company.

Yuval-Davis, Nira 1992: *Nationalism, Racism and Gender Relations.* The Hague: Institute of Social Studies. (Institute of Social Studies Working Paper No. 130).

Zarkov, Dubravka 2001: "The Body of the Other Man: Sexual Violence and the Construction of Masculinity, Sexuality and Ethnicity in the Croatian Media" in: Caroline O.N. Moser and Fiona C. Clark (eds.): *Victims, Perpetrators or Actors? Gender, Armed Conflict and Political Violence.* London: Zed Books.

Zdunnek, Gabriele 1997: Geschlechterverhältnisse in ethnischen Konflikten und Kriegen. *Peripherie* 17/68: 24–39.

Zdunnek, Gabriele 2002: "Akteurinnen, Täterinnen und Opfer – Geschlechterverhältnisse in Bürgerkriegen und ethnisierten Konflikten" in: Cilja Harders and Bettine Roß (eds.): *Geschlechterverhältnisse in Krieg und Frieden. Perspektiven der feministischen Analyse internationaler Beziehungen.* Opladen: Leske & Budrich.

Zimprich, Elke 1996: *Reintegration von Ex-Kämpferinnen in Eritrea. Eine gender-spezifische Studie in friedens- und entwicklungspolitischer Perspektive.* Hamburg: Institut für Afrika-Kunde.

Zisk Marten, Kimberly 2004: *Enforcing the Peace: Learning from the Imperial Past.* New York: Columbia University Press.

Zücher, Christoph 2004: "Einbettung und Entbettung: empirische institutionenzentrierte Konfliktanayse" in: Julie M. Eckert (ed.): *Anthropologie der Konflikte. Georg Elwerts konflikttheoretische Themen in der Diskussion.* Bielefeld: transcript Verlag.

Grey Literature

AMCO 2002: *Sierra Leone Diamond Policy Study*. London: Department for International Development [prepared by AMCO Robertson Mineral Services].

Boutros-Ghali, Boutros 1992: *An Agenda for Peace. Preventive Diplomacy, Peacemaking and Peace-Keeping.* Report of the Secretary-General <www.un.org/Docs/SG/agpeace.html> [15th September 2004].

Department for the Advancement of Women (DAW) 2000: *Gender Mainstreaming: Extract from Report of the Economic and Social Council for 1997 (A/52/3, 18 September 1997).* <www.un.org/womenwatch/daw/csw/GMS.PDF> [15th December 2004].

DDA 2001: *Gender Perspectives on Disarmament, Demobilisation and Reintegration (DDR).* Briefing Note 4. <www.disarmament2.un.org/gender/note4.pdf> [25th April 2005].

DDA 2003: *Department for Disarmament Affairs Gender Mainstreaming Action Plan.* Public Version. <http://disarmament2.un.org/gender/gmap.pdf> [23rd April 2005].

DDR 2003a: *The StopGap Programme.* DDR Coordination Section UNAMSIL. (Internal report)

DDR 2003b: *The DDR Process in Sierra Leone. Lessons Learned.* DDR Coordination Section UNAMSIL. (Unpublished report).

DDRR draft 2004: *Liberian Disarmament, Demobilisation, Rehabilitation and Reintegration Programme. Draft Strategy and Implementation Framework* by Draft Interim Secretariat. (Unpublished report).

IRIN 2005: *Sierra Leone: Blue Helmets Quit, but "Peace Elusive"*. United Nations Integrated Regional Information Networks on 14th December 2005. <www.irinnews.org/report.asp?ReportID=50685&SelectRegion=West_Africa&SelectCountry=SIERRA_LEONE> [15th December 2005].

Kai-Kai, Francis 2004: *NCDDR Meeting* (3rd February): Executive Secretariat Report. (Unpublished report).

Lomé Peace Agreement 1999: *Peace Agreement Between the Government of Sierra Leone and the Revolutionary United Front of Sierra Leone.* <www.sierra-leone.org/lomeaccord.html> [21st September 2004].

Marcaillou, Agnès 2004: *Gender Perspectives on D, D, and R. Conference Notes.* <www.womenwarpeace.org/issues/ddr/CSWgenderDDR.pdf> [25th April 2005].

National Consultation 2001: *Women and Men in Partnership for Post-Conflict Reconstruction.* Lagoonda Complex, Freetown on 21st–24th May 2001. (Unpublished report)

NCDDR 2002: *The DDR Programme: Status and Strategies for Completion. Executive Secretariat's Report for the Consultative Group Meeting. Paris.* (Internal report).

NCDDRR 2005: *DDRR Consolidated Report Phase 1, 2 & 3. Status of Disarmament and Demobilisation Activities as at 1/16/2005.* <www.humanitariinfo.org/Liberia/coordination/sectoral/DDR/doc/forthnightly%20report%207%20november%202004.pdf> [10th December 2005].

OSAGI 2002: *Gender Mainstreaming: an Overview.* Office of the Special Advisor to the Secretary-General on Gender Issues and Advancement of Women. New York: United Nations.

Schattenbericht 2003: *Schattenbericht zur Umsetzung von CEDAW in Deutschland.* <www.frauenrechte.de/pdf/1TeilSchattenbericht.pdf> [13th January 2005].

Schattenbericht 2004: *Schattenbericht zum Bericht der Bundesregierung Deutschlands über die Umsetzung der UN-Resolution 1325.* Vorgelegt vom Frauensicherheitsrat in Deutschland. <http://un1325.de/data/GLOW.pdf> [13th January 2005].

TRC report 2004: *Witness to Truth: Report of the Sierra Leone Truth & Reconciliation Commission.* <www.trcsierraleone.org> [10th December 2005].

UNHCR 1995: *Refugee.* 100(Special Focus: Refugee Women).

UNIFEM 2004: *Getting it Right, Doing it Right: Gender and Disarmament, Demobilisation and Reintegration.* New York: United Nations Development Fund for Women. <www.womenwarpeace.org/issues/ddr/gettingitright.pdf> [13th January 2005].

UNSC 1999: *United Nations Security Council Resolution 1270.* <http://daccessdds.un.org/doc/UNDOC/GEN/N99/315/02/PDF/N9931502.pdf?OpenElement> [3rd June 2004].

UNSG 2000: *The Role of United Nations Peacekeeping in Disarmament, Demobilisation and Reintegration.* Report of the Secretary General. <http://daccessdds.un.org/doc/UNDOC/GEN/N00/291/43/PDF/N0029143.pdf?OpenElement> [3rd June 2004].

UNSG 2004: *Twenty-first report of the Secretary-General on the United Nations Mission in Sierra Leone on 19th March 2004.* <http://daccessdds.un.org/doc/UNDOC/GEN/N04/270/25/PDF/N0427025.pdf?OpenElement> [3rd June 2004].

UNTAG 2000: *Windhoek Declaration" and "Namibia Plan of Action.* <www.glow-boell.de/media/de/txt_rubrik_2/WindhoekDecl(1).doc> [17th December 2004].

Wakhweya, Angela M., Catherine A. Rielley, Monica Onyango and Gail Helmer 2002: *HIV/AIDS, Gender and the Conflict Nexus: The Case of Sierra Leone. The Commoditization of Girls and Women.* (draft report for UNIFEM and UNFPA, July 2002).

Women's Commission for Refugee Women and Children 2002: *Disarmament, Demobilisation and Reintegration and Gender-Based Violence in Sierra Leone.* New York: Women's Commission for Refugee Women and Children.

7 Appendix

7.1 Interviews

Please note:

- The language in some interviews was a mix of English and Krio. If quoted directly, the translation into English is the author's. It will be specially marked if a third person was translating during the interview.
- For focus group discussions, the acronym of a related institution will be used to ease the referencing in the text. If quotes refer to a specific person within the group, a short characteristic shall be included in the reference within the text.
- In cases of only a given name appearing in the reference, the person requested anonymity.

Abu, Fatmata Kamara Kumba
Community elder, born 1914. She lost a brother in the war and was herself attacked but survived, using her age and status in *Bundu* as protection. Ms. Abu runs a *pojo*-hut[1] with her friend Mary Kamara, located next to a mass grave. Interview in Yengema on 21st June 2004.

Alice
Gender Advisor for an INGO working in Sierra Leone, which was implementation partner for UNAMSIL DDR Section. At the time of the fieldwork they are still involved in offering skills' training for ex-combatants. Alice comes from a francophone West African country and studied social sciences in Europe. Personal communication in Freetown on 3rd May 2004.

1 Place of gathering and consumption of *pojo*, palm wine.

Anna

Women's rights' activist working in the Liberian UN. Originally, she is from Sierra Leone and migrated to Europe and America during the time of tensions and war in her home country. Personal communication in Monrovia on 18th May 2004.

Conibere, Richard

Former data manager of the Truth and Reconciliation Commission for Sierra Leone. Originally a computer scientist from Great Britain, he has subsequently worked for the American Bar Association on a household-based survey of war-related human rights violations in Sierra Leone. Interview in Freetown on 6th May 2004.

CASTC

Group discussion with five women and four men ex-combatants participating in skills-training as part of DDR implemented by CASTC (local NGO) at the outskirts of Kailahun on 14th June 2004. The instructor translated specific Krio expressions.

CVT

Group discussion with local staff (three women and three men between the age of 25 and 32) of the Centre for Victims of Torture and affiliates in Kailahun Town on 14th June 2004. Some of them have been involved in the war, yet not all identify as ex-combatants. All of them have lived during the war in Kailahun District.

Elen

Liberian team leader of an INGO, working on SGBV and women's rights in a demobilisation camp. Interview in Liberia on 16th July 2004. She stressed that her observations are of a personal nature, not the NGO's.

Fatu

Former attack trader and involved in the civil war. Before the war, Fatu was a secretary in a catholic mission in Bo, where she married and had a son. She is now part of a women's income generation initiative in Kailahun. By continuing trade, she supports her husband and their two children. Interview in Kailahun on 16th June 2004.

FAWE Koidu
Group discussion with seven women ex-combatants aged between 17 and 28 in Koidu on 19th June 2004. Mrs. Princess Pratt, a local FAWE member, translated some Krio terms.

FAWE Yengema
Group discussion with eight women and two men ex-combatants aged between 22 and 31. Some of them have participated in DDR. Group Discussion in Yengema on 19th June 2004.

Foster, Joana
Senior Gender Advisor, UNMIL. In Ghana, her country of origin, Ms. Foster worked as a lawyer and in NGO-projects aiming at women's empowerment. Personal communication in Monrovia on 17th May and 14th July 2004.

Gbah, Elisabeth Dato
Works in the national headquarter of YWCA Liberia. She works for women's rights but emphasises that ideas of Western feminism are not convertible to (or desirable in) African societies. During the war, she stayed in Monrovia and tried to continue work with YWCA to support refugees seeking protection in the capital. Interview in Monrovia on 15th July 2004.

Wiles, Tonieh
Liberian activist for women's rights with a university background. She is now working for OXFAM as a gender and participation officer in West Africa. Interview in Monrovia on 16th May 2004.

Kai-Kai, Francis Dr.
Former Executive Secretary of NCDDR. Today, Dr. Kai-Kai is the Executive Secretary of the National Poverty Reduction Strategy Commission. Interview in Freetown on 3rd August 2004.

Kariatu
Formerly involved in the war herself, she is today working for an INGO in Kono, focussing on civil and human rights. She comes from an established background in Freetown and has attended secondary school. Interview in Koidu on 22nd June 2004.

Mr. Kalon
Community elder, *Poro* leader and "Justice of the Peace" in Bo District. Mr. Kalon has remained in Bo during the war and supported the CDF to defend the town. Participant in a UNIFEM workshop on Gender Justice in the legal system of Sierra Leone in Bo on 19th–21st April 2004.

Maria
SGBV Advisor for an INGO in Liberia, previously holding the same position in Sierra Leone. On the background of her work in the INGO, she is working on her PhD thesis at a British university. Interview in Monrovia on 15th July 2004.

Mbalu
She was captured by RUF/SL and stayed in two different camps lead by two different commanders throughout the war. Her mother was killed in the war; her brother's hands were amputated. Before the end of the war she was helped to escape with her child. Mbalu now works in a skills training project for community youth and ex-combatants and supports herself and her brother with this work. The interview took place with her friends and project participants Sarah and Margaret. These two sometimes commented or included their own perspectives. Both of them have been participating in different skills training projects before to earn a living. All three are in their mid 20's. Interview in Yengema on 21st June 2004.

MOCKY
Interview with the chair and two associates of the "Movement of Concerned Kono Youth", a local NGO addressing ex-combatants. The three men were fighting for RUF/SL and have created the organisation to support the marginalised former RUF/SL-members. Interview in Koidu on 22nd June 2004.

Momoh
Former local NGO staff in the reintegration programme for child combatants in the East and South of Sierra Leone. Before the war, Momoh worked as a secondary school teacher in Bo for more than 10 years. Interview in Freetown on 2nd May 2004.

Musa, Abu
Chair of the "Peace Pioneers Construction Group", an NGO working as implementation partner of UNAMSIL DDR section, which offers skills training to ex-combatants. Abu Musa also serves as Imam at a local mosque and includes religious reasons in his argumentation. Interview in Koidu on 21st June 2004.

Ngombeh, Jamba
Former RUF/SL "Minister for Education" in the "liberated areas", Ms. Ngombeh later served as liaison for the Disarmament and Demobilisation programmes in the districts of Kono and Kailahun. She belongs to a Ruling House in Kailahun District and is a prominent member of the community. Ms. Ngombeh now runs a pre-school programme supported by the local peacekeepers. Interview in Kailahun Town on 16th June 2004.

PRIDE
Group discussion with members of "Post-conflict Reintegration Initiative for Development and Empowerment" (PRIDE, local NGO addressing ex-combatants) in Freetown on 9th July 2004. All of the counterparts (three men and one women) come from an educated background and have themselves fought in the war.

Robert
Colonel from South-East Asia, presently MilOb in Liberia, previously in former Yugoslavia and Sierra Leone. In his home country, Robert teaches "Strategic Studies" and "Military History" at the military college. Interview in Freetown on 20th May 2004.

Robots, Victoria Finda
Local SGBV programme officer, COOPI Sierra Leone. The programme in Koidu is focussing on reproductive health and (S)GBV with women affected by the war. Interview in Koidu on 21st June 2004. She died in a helicopter crash on 29th June 2004.

Sajuma, Foday
CDF Commander in the Kailahun Region, now working with the local "Radio Moa", cooperation partner of Talking Drums Studios (INGO). He served as liaison officer during the DDR programme in Kailahun District, visiting the demobilisation camps with a colleague formerly fighting with RUF/SL, trying to support and encourage the ex-combatants. Interview in Kailahun Town on 18th June 2004.

Sheriff, Hawa
Female ex-combatant who demobilised with RUF/SL. Hawa has three children with her deceased (captor-) husband. At the time of the interview she was doing a skill-training course in metal works as part of the DDR. During this time, her children are with her mother, revealing family support, which she highly cherishes. Interview in Manowa on 17th June 2004.

Toweh, Roseline K.
National General Secretary of YWCA Liberia. The organisation is providing different services for women and girls affected by war, referring to them as "friends" rather than "(ex-)combatants". YWCA also plans to run skills training courses as part of the national DDR programme. Interview in Monrovia on 17th May 2004.

7.2 Map of fieldsites in Sierra Leone